MEET MY HEAD COACH

FRED CROWELL

All too often, we hold tenaciously to things precious in our lives. For me, it was basketball. Basketball is a great game; it is life in miniature. Like all other games, basketball cannot build character; it can only reveal one's character. Basketball is a poor God. God did not diminish my love for basketball but made my basketball bigger by teaching me how to use it as a tool for excellence in human behavior.

MEET MY HEAD COACH

FRED CROWELL

UPDATED
EDITION
with Current
Reflections

MEET MY HEAD COACH (Revision) © 2006 by Fred Crowell

MEET MY HEAD COACH (Original) © 1973 by The Moody Bible Institute of Chicago

ISBN: 0-8024-5225-6

Library of Congress Cataloging-In-Publications has been applied for.

The use of selected references from various versions of the Bible in this publication
does not necessarily imply publisher endorsement of the versions in their entirety.

Cover Design by Jesse Pierpoint, Pierpoint Design Branding, Spokane, WA

FRED'S REFLECTIONS ON THE UPDATED EDITION:
<u>MEET MY HEAD COACH</u>

People read books differently. Do you enjoy reading the preface or eagerly begin at the first chapter of the book? Are you one who reads the last chapter first or one who jumps from chapter to chapter? Do you savor each word or skim the book in one sitting? Or, just maybe, are you the clean reader, never highlighting or underlining?

Regardless of your reading preference, it is my deepest hope that you will experience more fully the joy of living as you read my discovery of my Head Coach. Why a reprint of the book with changes? It is because the life principles learned and presented here are as contemporary as yesterday. They transcend the ebb and flow of today's trends and fads, despite the changes in our world the past thirty-three years. These principles have formed the philosophy and teaching curriculum at NBC Camps.

The body of this book is in the exact format in which it was originally printed by Moody Press in 1973. However, this seventh printing will be a reprint with additions. The preface is written from a 2006 perspective. Each chapter begins with words from amazing people in my life who have been very important to my life journey; they are living proof to the claims that any ordinary person, like me, can accomplish dreams and goals beyond one's highest expectations when the Ultimate Coach weaves the extraordinary story. Pictures are included, hopefully worth a thousand words in this case. Finally, at the conclusion of each chapter is my brief reflection; looking back has given valuable perspective from a higher vantage point.

The one change is a new cover. Why hands holding a basketball? Basketball has been God's gift to me. Basketball is the tool God has given me to impact thousands of lives. However, the basketball needed to be held lightly and tenderly, as all created things on earth, lest they become our gods. My wish is that as you read how God has blessed my basketball, you will find He is waiting to bless what you are holding tenderly and carefully in your hands so that it becomes a tool to impact lives in a wonderful way.

My intent is not to change you. Rather, my intent is to be an encouragement in your life. My sincere desire is that you come as close as possible to living your fullest in this lifetime, for if we live well, we will most likely die well. It is my heartfelt conviction that in dying we truly begin to live.

To the three most important people in my life: my wife, Susie, and our two children, Jennifer and Jay, who live out daily the life principles communicated throughout the pages in "Meet My Head Coach." It is my conviction if one's philosophy of life does not work in the home, then it means little to share it with others. To these remarkable gifts, I am forever grateful. This is your book, dear family.

CONTENTS

FOREWORD

Reluctant? Recalcitrant? Resolved that the Christian life is not for you? So was Fred Crowell in 1965 and '66. His life plans were getting along very well under his own power. However, God had other plans for Fred. Gradually but unmistakably, He made His plans known and proceeded to implement them in spite of Fred's reluctance.

In *Meet My Head Coach*, Fred relates in a casual, attention-holding manner the changes in his life since Jesus Christ became his Head Coach and uses his experiences to encourage other skeptics to participate in the rich and satisfying life of one committed to Jesus Christ as Lord and Savior.

Throughout his book Fred makes clear the advantages of being practical with God. The Christian life, far from being a remote Utopian existence, offers a way to meet the realities of everyday life.

I first met Fred after his acceptance as a staff member of Campus Crusade for Christ where he served as coach of our Athletes in Action basketball team. Under his coaching and largely through his efforts, this team made a mighty impact for Christ wherever they played. It was my privilege to watch Fred himself grow and mature in Christ.

The principles Fred sets forth are not mere theories divorced from reality; they are principles hammered out on the anvil of life, lessons Fred learned in the front lines of spiritual combat. Fred's story describes in an entertaining and inspirational manner the practical benefits of making ourselves available to Jesus Christ to be used as He chooses.

For the non-Christian, *Meet My Head Coach* will provide convincing evidence that Jesus Christ is truly *"the way, the truth, and the life"* as He claimed (JOHN 14:6). For the Christian, it will kindle anew a desire to use his or her life to the maximum for the glory of God, which, after all, is the purpose for which we were created.

DR. BILL BRIGHT, FOUNDER
CAMPUS CRUSADE FOR CHRIST INTERNATIONAL

One of the most brilliant men I have known in my lifetime is the late Dr. Bill Bright. He was a master vision-builder with the wisdom to make the complex simple. Quite simply, Bill believed that God loves us and has a wonderful plan for our lives. When people know this truth, not only in their minds but also in their hearts, they can experience life in all its fullness. Personally, I am privileged to have been impacted by his life and to have his written Foreword. No one had more of a heart for God and this world in the twentieth century than did Dr. Bright.

Fred Crowell

FRED CROWELL

PREFACE

Several years ago, I met the former leader of a worldwide youth movement, and asked him a question I often ask people of wisdom: "What are two of the greatest surprises of your lifetime?"

After a few moments of reflection, this distinguished gentleman answered, "Of course, the incredible technological advancements in the last seventy years: man walking on the moon, the internet revolution, globalization....I could go on. It's truly unbelievable." He continued, "Secondly, it would have to be the moral decay and decline of our society; the crime, the drugs; the sheer moral bankruptcy that has taken hold. In fact, just the deterioration of society here in the United States in the last fifteen years has been unbelievable to me. Today, we have security guards in our schools; our jails are overcrowded with criminals; suicide is the second-leading cause of death among teens; and there is nothing short of a crisis in education. I remember growing up so eager to be educated. People prized getting a high school education. And a college education, well, that was the dream for most of us. Yet, today, thirty percent of our students drop out of high school. I stand amazed."

The enormous change society has undergone in the thirty-three years since I wrote *Meet My Head Coach* has been equally surprising to me. Needless to say, the world was a very different place then. Today, you only have to take a quick look around at the world we now live in to understand that there is a pressing need for the message of this book and others like it.

Writing the book all those years ago was challenging, no doubt. It was my first attempt at writing anything of any length, let alone a book. Just ask my high school English teachers; they will tell you, of all the students, I am one of the least likely to have ever written a book. The only reason I took English classes in college was to gain another teaching subject so that, ultimately, I would be able to coach basketball. Even with English classes under my belt, writing a book, for me, was like flying through the air – not just tricky, but practically impossible.

Yet, not only did I write it, but I did so in just one year. I was possessed. It was as though I had to write it. The words literally exploded from within me. My heart was so full of joy and passion that I simply had to share the life-changing message of my new head coach. Nor did I have any expectation that the finished product would be worthy of publication; I simply hoped, and prayed daily. I vividly recall the day the editor at Moody Press gave me the good news that *Meet My Head Coach* would be published. To me, it was a miracle. It proved to me once again, just as my four-year journey – my spiritual pilgrimage – had, that I could truly do all things through Christ who gives me the strength.

So, how did it all begin? We have to go back to one particular day in my coaching office when Fred Dyson, now a state senator in Alaska, asked me the most profound question I had ever been asked. "Coach," he said, "What do you think of the person, Jesus Christ?" The question literally blew my mind. I had no answer to it. No one had ever focused my attention on Jesus in this way. I had heard his name used in every conceivable manner, but never in the context of what he meant to me in a *personal* sense.

With this, I began to ask myself the all-important questions: Is there a God? Who is this God? What does this God want from me? Will this God be of any benefit to me in my life, in real terms? As I did, the prospect of a personal relationship with this God drew nearer. But – and it was a big "but" – my mother had died three years earlier from pancreatic cancer, the most brutal and terminal kind. Where was God in this? If there was a God, why did He not act? And what kind of relationship could I have with this sort of God? There began the most challenging journey of my entire life, as I was forced to reconcile two of life's greatest truths: the reality of God and the reality of death.

The key factor in this journey was the question of who I could trust to lead me. There is a saying: "If you don't stand for something, you'll fall for anything." Well, stand for something, yes; but make sure you choose *wisely* what you stand for. Just as when a jockey gets to ride in the Kentucky Derby, the key is to have a great horse; just as when a race driver gets one chance to drive the Indy 500, he had better have a great car. When you decide to follow a leader, you had better make a wise decision; because when it comes to leaders, the caliber of person you choose to follow will determine the kind of race you ultimately run.

Fortunately, I had the privilege of standing behind a great leader as a boy – my high school coach, Bill Taylor. Coach Taylor was a genius basketball coach. From my eighth grade year through high school, our team the Anacortes Seahawks won 115 out of 127 games. In five years, Anacortes lost just twelve games. In high school, I did whatever my wise coach asked. Coach said, "No hats in the building." I never wore a hat in the building. Coach said, "Get your hair cut short." I got my hair cut really short. Coach said, "No swearing, drinking alcohol, or getting in trouble with teachers, and get to bed early on school nights." I obeyed not only his no's, but his suggestions, too. Taylor was our god; he walked on water. And I believed if I did exactly what he told me to do, the team would win.

What was so special about Coach Taylor? And how did he help me to embrace my new head coach? First of all, after such a positive coaching experience in high school, I encountered the exact opposite in college, which left me well aware of the difference between a great head coach and a poor one. And when I decided, during my second year as head coach at the University of Alaska Fairbanks, to investigate the claims of Jesus Christ and His relevance to my life, I did so with this awareness. I knew the key to the question Fred Dyson asked me that day in 1966 was the reliability and trustworthiness of the leader. Naturally, the quality of the leader tells you a lot about the value of the message.

Secondly, what Coach Taylor did for me was nothing short of miraculous. He took a boy who had grown up with no male leadership whatsoever – a boy from a very poor home, a boy with no interior confidence, a boy who desperately needed structure – and turned him around. Because I could trust him, and believe in myself, I became a man. In fact, thanks to his leadership, I ended up with five major college scholarship offers. This is the genius of a great teacher. Anyone can point out your deficits and weaknesses; only the great ones can see your greatness before you see it yourself. And only the truly great ones can awaken this greatness. His faith in me, at a time when I had none in myself, gave me freedom. True leaders do exactly that; they set you free. They propel you towards becoming the person you are supposed to be.

But as good a man as Bill Taylor was for me, I still needed more. As great a head coach as he was to me, there was another head coach waiting to be discovered – one who could lead like no other, one who could provide for my needs like no one else could. And what I needed was no simple matter. I needed restoration of the mind, a renovation. I needed my life force to grow. I needed a new heart. I needed to know that one day I would see my blessed mother again. I needed to be freed from a bitter heart, from a life filled with rage and anger that began with an abusive father and the death of a wonderful mother. I needed a coach, a really good one. And I found this person, ultimately, in Jesus Christ.

Now, thirty-three years later, I am resurrecting this book. Why? Because I am adding a third surprise to the world youth leader's two surprises mentioned at the opening of the preface. I wrote this book in the early summer of my life. June is a great month in my part of the world. The sun is shining. Flowers are in bloom. It is a great time. I had dreams, lots of them; memories to make; worlds to conquer. It was easy for me to rise at four in the morning, drive from my home in Spokane, Washington, with the intent of stopping at every school possible until the day ended. In a single day, I would drive east to Montana through the panhandle of Idaho, Kellogg, Wallace, Mullan, St. Ignasius, Ronan, Big Fork and Kalispel, and then stay overnight with a friend who loved me enough to give me shelter and food because I had little money; the next day I would discover a new route home to make new friends in my dream to have the greatest basketball camp in the world.

Now in the winter season of my life – hopefully, very early winter – I have discovered that I am more effective working with young people as a grandfather figure than as a supercharged, high-energy, skillful 30-year-old basketball coach capable of defeating any of my students on the basketball court. I can no longer impress them with my physical skills. I can no longer outwork all of my young coaches; or, for that matter, care about who is best or better, or who wins or loses. What I can do, though, is listen better, be more compassionate, demonstrate kindness at every opportunity, enjoy the success of others with greater humility, seek a gentle spirit, and live in the joy that flows from a greater measure of patience.

Today, I am different, and I do things differently. The world, too, is different today than it was yesterday. This means the book is bound to have a different impact – perhaps a more powerful one. Just as more explosive material produces a more powerful blast, the decline of our society means an even greater impact for Jesus. It is my firm conviction that the story is more relevant today than it was thirty-three years ago. People need to know that God truly loves them and has a wonderful, remarkable plan for their lives.

Thankfully, people are still reading the book. They are still finding Christ in it. Given this, the passage of time, and my personal evolution, I am hopeful that this book might strike a different but equally resonant chord with new readers. If the book speaks to you better than it could have thirty-three years ago, just as I have learned to listen better than I used to; if it quenches a thirst it could not have quenched before; if it satisfies a hunger that did not exist before, then I have every reason in the world to resurrect it.

MEET **MY**
HEAD
COACH

1

A DOLLAR TODAY, LORD?

"

"Don't be afraid that your life will end; be afraid that it will never begin." ANONYMOUS

The beginning of my life was spent in fear of death. This fear drove me to Jesus. I looked alive to others—I was a college graduate, a teacher (a profession I still enjoy), and in good health. I married my college sweetheart, and he adored me as much as I loved him. On the surface, there was nothing that showed the great fear I felt. My fears were exacerbated by the death of my husband's mother and also one of my dear students.

At the end of myself, I heard about Jesus and began a relationship with Him in July, 1965. I found life in Him. *"But because of His great love for us, God, who is rich in mercy, made us alive with Christ even when we were dead in transgressions—it is by grace you have been saved"* (EPHESIANS 2:4).

After coming to know Jesus, I was a new person. Every truth in this book is possible only through Jesus loving and working in our lives. The truths presented are a gift of grace. He sends His Word, many special teachers and friends to love and guide us along the way. Most importantly, He gives us Himself. *"I have come that they may have life, and have it to the full"* (JOHN 10:10).

We continue to learn the lessons of this book, and many more, but that is a story for another book. We continue to grow in His grace daily. When you read the book, may you see Jesus glorified on every page and in every story. We give Him all the praise and glory for our journey. Great things He has done and continues to do daily. *"Because of the Lord's great love we are not consumed, for His compassions never fail. They are new every morning; great is Your faithfulness"* (LAMENTATIONS 3:22-23).

SANDRA S. CROWELL

SANDRA "SUSIE" CROWELL LIVES IN SPOKANE, WASHINGTON, WITH FRED AND WITHIN THREE MINUTES WALKING DISTANCE OF HER BEAUTIFUL GRANDDAUGHTERS' HOME. SHE HOLDS TWO MASTER'S DEGREES FROM GONZAGA UNIVERSITY, IN SPIRITUALITY AND COUNSELING PSYCHOLOGY. FOR OVER THIRTY YEARS, SUSIE HELD SEVERAL POSITIONS WITH NBC CAMPS AND NOW IS AN ADJUNCT TEACHER AT EASTERN WASHINGTON UNIVERSITY.

I f I am going to trust God with my soul when I die, I want to be able to trust God for a dollar today! It is amazing to hear people explain that they expect to enjoy eternity in heaven with God and find they refuse to trust this God, who is going to raise them from the dead, for simple everyday details. Since the almighty dollar is closest to most hearts, this is a great test of a man's faith.

Jesus said, *"Look at the birds of the air; they do not sow or reap or store away in barns, and yet your heavenly Father feeds them. Are you not much more valuable than they?...And why do you worry about clothes? See how the lilies of the field grow. They do not labor or spin. Yet I tell you that not even Solomon in all his splendor was dressed like one of these....your heavenly Father knows that you need them"* (MATTHEW 6:26,28,29,32).

My philosophy for the past seven years has been to be as practical as possible with God. If I cannot trust Him for a dollar today, I certainly do not want to trust Him with my soul for eternity. But to be perfectly frank, the decision to set my lifestyle according to this fundamental principle of Christian living came about more by chance than by design. Let me tell you about it.

My entire life has revolved around athletics. I believe this has created my deep desire to face life in a practical manner. I have found that it does little good to dream or theorize, because the proof of a successful athlete is in his performance. Some folks talk a great game and are the finest locker room players alive, but in the heat of the battle they are nowhere to be found.

Early in my school life, a group of classmates and I vowed to win the state basketball championship when we became seniors. Our small community in Anacortes, Washington, had never had a state champion, though it had many great basketball teams. But vow or not, our team placed third in the state playoffs. We were beaten in a very close game in the semifinals by the team that went on to win the championship. As our team ran onto the court before 13,000 fans, I realized that many years of dreaming were not going to do the job. Ten or twelve years were condensed into thirty-two minutes of basketball. This was where the proverbial tennis shoe met the hardwood, and we were faced with reality, not dreaming.

For as long as I can remember, basketball and baseball were the very reasons for living. At an early age I became committed to athletics and knew that one day I would enter the coaching profession. My desire to face life in a practical, logical manner was reinforced when all this dedication and hard work was rewarded by a college basketball scholarship. My academic schedule also challenged me to face the realities of life.

My years in college taught me other things about reality. I began to realize that my Sunday morning in church had nothing to do with the other 167 hours of my week. In my quest to succeed, I wanted to use time wisely, so Sunday morning became a time to catch up on sleep. My goal was to be a successful coach, and I simply could not draw a correlation between that and sitting in church. Observation and experience verified this philosophy.

At the conclusion of my junior year, two momentous events occurred. The first was one of the happiest experiences of my life. My high school friends had predicted that I would be the first to get married since I refused to get involved with girls and warned them about marrying at an early age. They were right! I was the first to get married, and it was love at first sight.

The second experience was the greatest tragedy of my life. My mother died of cancer. It was an agonizing experience. Each day I visited her at the hospital and watched her waste away. Since I could not solve this problem myself, I reverted to my earlier belief in God and repeatedly asked Him to help my mother. When she died I became very bitter toward religion and thoroughly convinced God did not rule in the hearts and lives of men, as some contended. I never went so far as to say there was not a God, because I was not in a position to have that knowledge, but it no longer mattered to me whether there was a God or not. I could not reconcile an all-powerful God with the misery He had allowed my family to experience. This experience was especially difficult for me because I had always been able to work things out to make bleak situations look bright. Yet in this situation, I was helpless to even that.

To add to my bitterness, I was confronted by a clergyman before my mother's funeral and told in no uncertain terms that I had better get right with God. This was not the time to confront me with religion. I decided that when the funeral was over I would not darken the door of the church again.

My goals in life were to be successful, to be honest with myself, and to help other people. If by some remote chance there was a God, I would be OK because God would weigh my good deeds against my bad deeds, or so I reasoned.

In the following years, several of my friends tried to influence me to join their particular brand of religion. But I thought religion was a figment of man's imagination and was not interested. To me successful living was being faithful to my responsibilities and doing my tasks well. This approach to life paid off handsomely. I did well in my master's degree program, in coaching the frosh basketball team, and while serving as head resident-hall advisor at a men's dormitory during my fifth year in college.

The biggest break of my life came when I accepted the position of head basketball coach at the University of Alaska. This was an unbelievable opportunity. I was just twenty-three years old. Hard work and dogged determination were still my guidelines, and in my first year at the university we posted a 13-3 record. This was the first winning season in the history of the school.

But an even more remarkable event took place. My wife, Susie, taught in Fairbanks, Alaska. One day while driving to school, Susie experienced intense chest pain, which led her to believe she might be having a heart attack. After a thorough examination at the hospital, the doctor assured her it was not a heart attack. He could find no reason for the pain but felt rest and relaxation would solve the problem.

These chest pains continued periodically throughout the spring, however. Rest, relaxation, and medication did not solve the problem. We thought a summer of fun in Oregon, California, Washington, and Idaho would be just the answer. We traveled as far as Portland, Oregon and were planning to have lunch with a relative, when Susie had another attack. As she was experiencing intense pain, we enlisted the services of a physician. After an examination, the doctor said Susie had a type of fibrillation of the heart, a condition where the muscles around the heart tighten and do not allow it to beat freely. The result is great pain.

The doctor asked us many questions regarding our marriage, financial solvency, sexual relations, jobs, and so on. Both of us were perfectly content in all areas of marriage and profession and were doing well financially. The doctor simply could not understand why Susie was having difficulty. A short time later I learned that a famous medical clinic in the United States confirmed that eighty-two percent of all their cases are psychosomatic. This may be why it is so common for doctors to have difficulty determining the exact cause of certain illnesses.

Susie and I continued south, enjoying the countryside and looking for possible basketball players to venture to the frozen northland to play for the University of Alaska. We had great times with close friends, enjoyed the sights of northern California, and had three enjoyable days at Disneyland. In spite of all our wonderful, carefree times, Susie continued to have periodic bouts of severe chest pains. I was determined to send her through a clinic of medical experts as soon as we got back to her hometown area, but Susie wanted to see her childhood physician first. I was opposed because I was tired of small-town doctors and also because, at that time, I questioned a female doctor. (It is amazing to me how years ago many of us thought about gender.) But for some unexplainable reason, Susie wanted to see this doctor she had not seen for several years.

Shortly after lunch on a beautiful July afternoon in northern Idaho, Susie walked to the doctor's office while I banged plastic golf balls off the side of the house. Three hours passed and Susie had not returned. It was extremely difficult to concentrate on golf practice, and I found myself looking down the street in the direction of the doctor's office every few minutes. Finally, I saw my little lady walking up the street, and I raced to meet her. I pressed for an explanation and was somewhat bewildered when Susie said she wanted to wait to talk with me in the house. My mind was filled with all sorts of fears as I anticipated some dreadful news.

We proceeded into the house, and I was directed to sit down. Susie also took a seat and solemnly reported the doctor's diagnosis. "After an extensive examination, the doctor tells me there is nothing physically the matter with me," Susie said.

"What is wrong then?" I asked, confused because good news should not require such elaborate preparation.

"The doctor believes I have a spiritual problem which can only be solved by God," Susie quietly replied.

Wow, I got heated real fast. What nerve! How could an M.D. possibly peddle that kind of garbage in the name of medicine? I wanted to know what medical school taught such nonsense!

I asked the most obvious question, "What are you going to do about it?"

"The doctor wants us to see a minister," Susie replied.

"Us? You must be dreaming, Susie. I'm not going to see any minister." As far as I was concerned, a minister should confine himself to two jobs, weddings and funerals.

The more I talked with Susie, the more I realized I was between a rock and a hard place. Here was the wife I loved more than anything in the world, asking me to have a private meeting with a minister. I had always thought I would do anything for her, but I had never dreamed of this. Realizing Susie's intense desire to follow through, I said I would go with her, but I did not say I would be nice.

The next afternoon we trudged off to see our minister "friend." We were ushered into a small office. A big black Bible, which immediately made me uneasy, was open on the desk, but through the years I had become an expert in religious argument and thought I would have one going in a short time. Much to my amazement, I could not get an argument started with this man. Regardless of my question, he simply turned to the Bible and let it answer. I had to admit I was impressed, but I certainly was not ready to swallow everything hook, line, and sinker; so I left the room and went outside to wait for Susie.

About a half hour later, Susie came out to where I was standing by the car and said something that I will never forget.

"Fred, I want you to know that I really love you. Today something wonderful has happened to me; I just invited Jesus Christ to come into my life to be my Savior and Lord. Someday I want you to make this wonderful discovery."

I did not know exactly what she meant. Was my wife going to become some religious fanatic? I was content with the way things were and did not want to have anything changed. But I could see the obvious joy in Susie's face and, in a way, was happy for her.

Since I was once the biggest skeptic alive, I certainly do not blame anyone for being skeptical. For those who question the validity of this experience, all I can say is that Susie has not had any type of chest pain since that July afternoon in 1966. Call it hocus-pocus, mind over matter, or anything else; all I know is that receiving Jesus Christ into her life worked, and it cost me not a dime. To my way of thinking, it was a far better stroke of business than shelling out money to doctors who did not alleviate the problem. Do not misunderstand me, I am not down on the medical profession. On the contrary, I am a strong advocate and rely upon their services. However, in this case, I saw Jesus Christ meet a tangible need.

I have gotten ahead of myself, since at this stage of the game we did not know if these chest pains would disappear permanently, and I was a long way from ready to give God credit for anything.

That evening I read the gospel of John before going to bed because the minister had challenged me to do so. There, he said, I could find out if there was a God I could know personally. The lights did not come on for me; however, I agreed to attend church with my wife during our remaining time in Idaho before returning to Alaska to begin our second year.

I saw a quality of life that I admired in the people attending this church. I saw warmth, compassion, and a genuine concern for other people. I even enjoyed the minister's messages because he did not give his opinions of the Vietnam War, major in the negatives, or harp on the do's and don'ts of being a Christian, but simply opened the Bible and stuck to what God had to say. I was beginning to soften but was still miles away from making a decision for Christ.

....

Current Reflections

To buy in, it had better be good! For me to buy in, it had to be better than good; ultimately, I wanted the best. All religion and philosophy are selling something. As in all sales, I had to ask, what are you selling? What is it going to cost? Will the price be worth it?

Also, as in all decisions, I had three choices: Yes, I will buy; no, I will not buy; or I will walk away without making a decision. Most often, two of the three choices are poor ones. Little did I know at that time that when it comes to choosing a head coach for life, the third option would make me the head coach.

Choosing a trustworthy head coach for my life was the most difficult decision I could face. It made perfect sense that if God was not trustworthy in every area of my life on a daily basis, then trusting Him on my deathbed was illogical. Was it possible to know God? If so, could He, and would He, govern in the affairs of my life? This was my ultimate concern.

In 1966, I knew this choice was going to cost me everything. Today, forty years later, I know it was worth it. Without question, the Head Coach I chose was the best and most important decision of my life. The second most important coach in my life, Susie, was instrumental in this decision.

Chapter Notes

MEET MY
HEAD
COACH

2

PREACHER, I'LL BE THE SKEPTIC

"

Fred Crowell has always been an intense man who wanted to win at whatever he was doing. I have always thought of him as the "Go-for-it Guy." In reality, the University of Alaska basketball team practices in 1966 were far tougher than their games. Personally, I have played scores of hours of "pick-up" basketball with Fred, and they were all tough! When he decided to drive to the basket, he was going to put the ball in the basket no matter what! Without question, if I was guarding him, I was going to get run over and maybe hurt.

Fred brings that kind of decisiveness to all aspects of life. When I first approached him in 1966 at the University of Alaska, he gave no hint of any personal lacks, crises, or needs. This was undoubtedly his way of dealing with his childhood. Nonetheless, the changes in his wife's life, the draw of truth and Christ's love, all pushed him to seek more about Christ.

When Fred realized God loved him individually and unconditionally, he committed himself to pursue the newly found lover of his soul. Out of the pursuit of this relationship, he has been able to form life principles which encourage me even today. Some of these principles are:

- Got a problem with a person? It's your move. You cannot change others; you can only change yourself to improve a relationship.
- Be purposeful—move towards your goals. If change is going to happen, it takes a concerted plan and action over time.
- Most people want to win; few will prepare to win. Excellence and success require "dogged" practice and preparation.

It is a great privilege to have seen a seed, sown on fertile ground, bear much delightful truth.

FRED DYSON

FRED DYSON HAS REMARKABLE LOYALTY AS A FRIEND. HE AND HIS WIFE, JANE, HAVE THREE MARRIED CHILDREN AND SEVEN GRANDCHILDREN. TOGETHER THEY LIVE IN EAGLE RIVER, ALASKA. FOR THE PAST TEN YEARS, FRED HAS SERVED AS A SENATOR FOR THE STATE OF ALASKA. PREVIOUSLY, HE WAS EMPLOYED AS A MECHANICAL ENGINEER.

At the end of the summer, Susie and I went back to Fairbanks eager to begin another school year. I was impressed with my wife's happiness and joy in being a Christian and, because of her happy life, wondered if Christ was for real. We tried several churches when we got back to Fairbanks, but I remained unconvinced.

One day while sitting in my office at the university, preparing for basketball practice, a sharp young man approached me, introduced himself as Fred Dyson, and told me that he worked for Campus Crusade for Christ. Fred hit it off with me immediately, because he said he was interested in my team and wanted to see us do well. I was for anyone who followed my team. We had a great time talking about athletics.

Fred had graduated from the University of Washington in engineering and had rowed on their outstanding crew team. Fred shared a booklet with me called The Four Spiritual Laws, and we talked about Christianity.

The following week Susie and I invited Fred and his wife, Jane, to visit us one evening. It was an unusual evening for us, because we did not play cards or draw basketball plays, a custom always exercised in our home with guests. Instead we talked about the person of Jesus Christ. It was one of the most refreshing and enjoyable evenings we had ever spent. After Fred and Jane left our home, we were in high spirits because we had done something we had never thought possible, and it was so enjoyable.

That Friday evening was a turning point in my life because the Dysons had invited us to attend a newly organized church with them the following Sunday. It was everything a church should not be according to my religious upbringing. The first service was held in the minister's home. Chairs were crowded into one corner and a record player provided the special music. In spite of these surroundings, I was strongly attracted by the sincerity and warmth of the people.

Within a very short time, the church outgrew the pastor's living room, and the Carpenters' Hall became the meeting place. This did not add much to the aesthetic values, but the radiance and joy continued to be present.

I had made no decisions, and this was quite obvious to everyone. I looked for hypocrisy and inconsistency but could find none. My hang-up was this business of faith. My conscience would not allow me to take a flying leap into uncertainty.

Believing the unbelievable was as illogical as jumping out the window of a ten-story building and expecting to come out of the fall unharmed. Exercising faith would be committing intellectual suicide.

One Sunday morning, the minister announced that the following week there would be a panel discussion on "Why Believe in the Bible." He wanted two volunteers to be skeptics and two more to defend the Bible. No one volunteered, and I began to feel sorry for the pastor. Trying to be a nice guy, I raised my hand and said, "Pastor, I'll be a skeptic." My good friend and frosh basketball coach at the university, Lee Cassel, was sitting next to me and offered to be a skeptic with me. I sat there relaxed, poised, and chuckling to myself, because I knew this certainly would not require much preparation. Suddenly Peter Three Star, a 275-pound Sioux Indian who worked with the Bureau of Indian Affairs, raised his hand and volunteered to be a skeptic "if Crowell will defend the Bible."

The audience was delighted, and the minister was all smiles, but I was beginning to perspire. For some reason, I did not refuse. I just did not have the courage to jump up and say no. I was about to defend something I did not believe. In fact, I had only read one book of the entire Bible. Oh, I had also read some of the Psalms since I had to begin the day with a Bible reading when I was a student teacher in English. Of course, I always selected the shortest Psalm I could find. I was ignorant about the Bible and what the Bible contained.

Needless to say, I heard nothing of the remainder of the morning service. When we went outside after the service was over I said, "Susie, what in the world am I going to do?" Her reply was, "I don't know, but it sure is going to be interesting."

Evaluating my position, two alternatives came to mind—study or just don't show up. The second was the most appealing, but I knew this would not be the thing for the head basketball coach of the university to do. Several of my players would be there, and it would be a disgrace to stay home.

As I look back on this portion of my life, I realize two experiences were of monumental value. The first significant one took place as I drove home from church. In my nervous state I turned on the car radio. I heard a speaker say that everyone had a basic desire to believe in someone greater than himself. This is faith. Insight! The lights came on; faith was the key to life! The successful coach was the one who could instill faith in his men so they believed they could reach greater heights than ever imagined. This phenomenon of faith explains why an inferior team can defeat a much superior team on any given day.

The previous two years I had been the head resident-hall advisor, one year at the University of Idaho and another at the University of Alaska. Over fifty percent of the boys in both my dorms flunked out of college. It was disheartening to counsel with so many young men who had no desire or purpose in life because of their lack of faith. It was definitely true that those with the most severe problems had no faith, not even in themselves.

Initially I had thought dormitory counseling to be such a good deal that I persuaded a friend to take a similar position at a neighboring dorm. He had an unforgettable year. One student nearly shot another to death, another tried to kill himself with a gun, still another slashed his wrists with glass. What do you tell a young fellow who has just attempted to take his own life? What advice do you give a collegian who not only hates the world but despises himself? I did not have the answers. All of these experiences helped me realize that without faith in something, man has severe problems.

This all fell into place as I drove home from church. I wrote seven or eight pages on the subject of faith. The more I thought about man's need for faith, the more I realized the importance of believing in God. The primary reason for this conclusion stemmed from my utter inability to motivate those with no personal motivation even though I was very effective in working with those who had a desire to achieve. For the student who just did not care about life, I had no answers.

Writing this treatise on faith became an effective tool toward overcoming frustration with my inability to help students in severe difficulty. I was unable to help others in need because of inconsistency in my own philosophy; I was wrong in assuming man was innately good. St. Augustine was correct when he said that God has created us for Himself and our hearts restless until we find our rest in Him. To prove his point, all I had to do was observe the people around me. Now I needed to know how to find God.

This brings me to the second experience which proved helpful during this crisis hour.

The previous semester I had taught a course called the history of physical education. To teach it effectively, I had to know something about the religious beliefs of various countries. I learned Hinduism has a marked effect on physical education in India; the polytheism of Greece greatly influenced the lives of their athletes; nearly every religious system has ideas regarding man's body. As a result, physical education will either prosper or suffer depending on a culture's religious philosophy.

Now, in preparation for Sunday's debate, I decided to go to the university library and find out what Christianity had to offer, and Fred Dyson brought me a stack of books to study. As I studied, I found more than I set out to. I was amazed at the unique claims of Christianity. I discovered that Jesus Christ was the only man who ever claimed to be God and substantiated His claims. He did not claim to be a prophet, as Moses, Elijah, Muhammad, Buddha, and others did. He claimed to be the Christ, the Messiah, the one who transforms lives and forgives sins.

Mahatma Gandhi in *All Men Are Brothers* says, *"The only virtue I want to claim is truth and non-violence. I lay no claim to super-human powers. I want none. I wear the same corruptible flesh that the weakest of my fellow-beings wear and am liable to err as any. My services have many limitations, but God has up to now blessed them in spite of the imperfections."* In contrast, Jesus said, *"Know that the Son of man has authority on earth to forgive sins"* **(MARK 2:10)**.

Realizing that Jesus claimed to be God, I became aware that there are three possibilities when we consider who Jesus Christ really is. Jesus had to be one of the following—liar, lunatic, or God. As C. S. Lewis, Professor at Oxford University, who denied the deity of Christ for many years, so aptly stated, "A man who was merely a man and said the sort of things Jesus said would not be a good moral teacher. He would either be a lunatic—on the level of the man who says he is a poached egg—or else he would be the devil of hell. You must make your choice. Either this man was and is the Son of God, or else a madman or something worse. You can shut Him up for a fool; you can spit at Him or kill Him as a demon; or you can fall at His feet and call Him Lord and God."

For the first time in my life, I realized that the key to Christianity is Jesus Christ. Christianity is a relationship, not a religion or code of ethics. If you take Christ out of Christianity, you have nothing left. This is not true of other religions of the world. On the basis of evidence at hand, I was sure Jesus was not a liar or a lunatic, but He was in fact God.

In the areas of archaeology, and prophecy, I came across startling facts that verified the intellectual tenability of Christianity. In high school and college I had read Homer's Iliad and Odyssey, Plato's Republic, and many other excellent literary masterpieces. None of my teachers ever questioned the authorship or authenticity of those manuscripts. Some of these teachers had little regard for the reliability, authorship, or authenticity of the New Testament. Yet from an archaeological standpoint, the Gospels of the New Testament are held in high regard. I am confident there is more evidence for the reliability of the New Testament manuscripts than evidence that Homer ever lived, let alone wrote the Iliad and the Odyssey.

Dr. William F. Albright, the late professor emeritus of Johns Hopkins University, said, "There can be no doubt that archaeology has confirmed the substantial historicity of the Old Testament tradition."

Nelson Glueck, renowned Jewish archaeologist, made this remarkable statement, "It may be stated categorically that no archaeological discovery had ever controverted a Biblical reference."

William F. Albright, another great archaeologist, stated, "The excessive skepticism shown toward the Bible by important historical schools of the eighteenth and nineteenth centuries, certain phases of which still appear periodically, has been progressively discredited. Discovery after discovery has established the accuracy of innumerable details, and has brought increased recognition to the value of the Bible as a source of history."

Finally, I began to evaluate the Bible by looking through the concordance. I read where the Bible had profound things to say about jealousy, bitterness, selfishness, and inferiority. I thought, almost in a naïve way, that if I could know this material well enough, I could really help college students who were having so much trouble with these very things.

The greatest discovery I made that week of preparation was that it is wrong to say you just have to take a big, flying leap of faith into the unknown to experience God through the person of Jesus Christ. I came up with so much factual information on the life, death, and resurrection of Jesus Christ that intellectually I knew he had to be God. Reliable faith must be based on fact. In the book of Hebrews the author tells us that *"Now faith is being sure of hoped what we hope for and certain of what we cannot see"* (HEBREWS 11:1). I believe there is very little we do in life that does not require faith, because anything that involves the future requires faith.

Let me explain through a simple illustration how faith must be based on fact in order to be logically sound.

One of my basketball players approaches me and needs to borrow $100 because he is in a bind; but he assures me he will return the money in two weeks. I'm sure nearly anyone in this situation would loan this close friend the money, if he had it to loan. On the other hand, a perfect stranger approaches me, asks to borrow $100, and promises to return it in two weeks. Few would loan money under these circumstances.

Both situations involve faith. How do you know for sure your money will be returned in two weeks? In both situations, faith is necessary. It is not hard for me to loan my player $100 because I know him and have confidence in his character; therefore, I loan him the money by faith based on the facts of my previous experiences with him. But since I have no facts about the other man, I have no faith in him. Likewise, when I give my life over to Christ and ask Him to be my Savior and Lord, I need facts upon which to hang my faith.

As I prepared to defend the Bible, I realized it took a far greater leap of faith not to commit my life to Christ than it did to accept Him into my life. Intellectually and logically I did not have a choice. If I wanted to be honest with myself, I had to acknowledge Jesus Christ as my Savior.

By showing that faith is reasonable and based on fact, I do not mean to imply that faith is not important. Faith is God's method of blessing people. You will see this later on in chapters to follow. In fact, when I became a Christian, I prayed something like this, "OK, Christ, I realize that You are God, and if You can change my life, I want You to do just that. But I want You to be the most practical experience of my life. I don't want this to be a Sunday morning, phony-baloney affair. I want to experience You in my coaching, teaching, marriage, and relationships with other people." This required faith on my part.

This was possibly the most important prayer of my life because I discovered that Jesus Christ answers specific prayer. Immediately, I began to experience evidence of Christ changing my life. One of the first challenges I gave Him was to take the habit of swearing away. For years I had tried different methods and gimmicks to eliminate this distasteful quality. It was gratifying to see God work in this area. Temper and impatience were others. I had excellent control of my outward appearance, but much of the time was upset with circumstances. I could become angry following an inept driver, or getting caught in a traffic jam, or not having things go my way. I asked the Lord to give me peace and patience and experienced results which caused me to want Him in other areas of my life.

I owe a lot to that big Sioux Indian for having the courage to challenge me to defend the Bible. He was easy on me during the panel discussion; in fact, everyone was extremely polite and courteous. I am sure they were delighted to see me taking a positive stand for the Bible. But even without Peter Three Star making it easy for me, Lee Cassel and I could have commanded the situation. God has a lot to say, and we experienced forcefulness in reading His answers.

After the panel discussion ended, everyone was happy. Peter was happy because Lee and I had won the debate; the pastor was happy because he had one less skeptic, and I was happy because I no longer needed to play the role of a non-believer.

Project 1

- Have you made the discovery of knowing Jesus Christ personally?

  Yes___ No___ Not Sure___

- On page 144 of the appendix is the Four Spiritual Laws by Dr. Bill Bright. This practical presentation will take you only a few minutes to read. Do this now.

- Read 2 Corinthians 5:17. If you read the Four Spiritual Laws and invited Jesus Christ into your life, thank God that you are now a new creature in Christ.

Current Reflections

There have been many times in my life when my faith has been challenged. At the age of twenty-one, my faith in God crumbled when my mother died of pancreatic cancer. Why?

When my dear friend, Chuck Hepworth, died of multiple melanoma cancer twenty years after my mother's death, my faith in God grew stronger. Why?

Faith is a fact of life and is based on fact. Everyday we exercise faith. The more facts we have, the more faith we have. Daily we perform tasks which require faith. A person who has never seen an airplane may find it impossible to believe the plane can fly like a bird. Yet the frequent flier boards the plane without the slightest doubt the plane will reach its targeted destination.

The reason my faith in God crumbled at my mother's death is directly related to the fact that I did not have any facts to hang my hat of faith upon. My perspective changed when I learned the illustration that the engine of the train is fact, while the fuel tank is faith, and the caboose is feeling. My problem was that my feelings were the engine of my life at the time of my mother's death.

Yet when Chuck Hepworth went through the valley of the shadow of death, I was equipped with the necessary faith to deal with the agony and pain because I had fed my faith with facts, thereby starving my doubts based on feelings. Facing death made me realize love and suffering go hand in hand. It is not possible for a mother to bring a child into the world without suffering. It is not possible to parent children with deep love and joy without suffering when they leave home. It is not possible to live fully until we are willing to die; when we are willing to die, we can fully embrace life. The key then is not letting life's suffering destroy our faith, but using our faith to buoy us through life's suffering.

Chapter Notes

Chapter Notes

MEET **MY**
HEAD
COACH

3

A TWO-WAY STREET

"

When it comes to the what, the why, and the how of being a Christian, Fred Crowell has put together a masterpiece of simple and direct truths that inform and inspire.

As a high school senior basketball player on the number-one-ranked team in the state of Washington, my older sister gave me a book for Christmas by Fred Crowell titled *Meet My Head Coach*. At that time I did not know who Fred Crowell was, but I was into basketball so I dug into the book. It was basketball and so much more as Fred shared his story. Although I am sure I must have heard the concept as a church-going child, this was the first time the idea of a personal relationship with Jesus Christ and what it meant had been presented so clearly. Of course, as a senior I knew everything about everything, and my life was going great. Still, I identified with the spiritual need Fred explained and asked Jesus into my life after reading the book. That act started me on a journey of growth and friendships which have enriched my life and given me perspective and hope through life's challenges and victories.

As a college student, a friend invited me to coach basketball at a camp near Spokane, Washington. The experience was awesome, and, unbeknownst to me at the time, the founder of that camp was the same Fred Crowell whose book had changed my life. Over the years, that same NBC Camps has had an enormously positive impact on my family and me, and I personally have seen the impact on hundreds more.

I am a living testimony to the fact that if a person steps out in faith and embraces the concepts presented in this book, it will result in a life changed for the better. I am eternally grateful to Fred for sharing his life in this way.

ROGER DORWAY

ROGER DORWAY IS A BUSINESS CONSULTANT IN WEST LINN, OREGON, WHERE HE LIVES WITH HIS WIFE, JANA, AND FOUR CHILDREN: WHITNEY, SPENCER, RILEY, AND HANNAH. HE IS A GRADUATE OF EVERETT HIGH SCHOOL AND WASHINGTON STATE UNIVERSITY.

I did not realize when I asked Christ to be practical that this was a two-way street. He brought situations into my life that forced me to be practical. One night at basketball practice, Fred Dyson appeared. Very casually he asked if I would be able to talk to a few students. Noticing that Fred was hedging, I pressed him to tell me what I was to speak about. He told me I could choose my subject. I said, "Don't give me that, Dyson, you want me to talk about Christ." All I got for an answer was a big smile. "OK, I'll do it, but when is this big event?" I really pushed the panic button when he said, "Oh, in about two hours."

Speaking to forty college students about the reality of Jesus Christ in my life was a big challenge. I thanked God for this opportunity to put my faith on the line. Several basketball players and many students expressed their appreciation after my talk. This meant a great deal to me.

My second encounter took place in Anchorage, Alaska where I was participating in a teachers' conference and also teaching a basketball clinic. One evening, I received a call in my hotel room. It was Fred Dyson inviting Susie and me to attend a banquet with him. Unfortunately, we were already committed to attend another banquet. No sooner had I hung up the telephone than there was a knock at the door. When we opened it, Fred was standing there. Sheepishly he explained that he had telephoned from the lobby, not from across town as he had led us to believe. He wanted me to come downstairs and say a few words to a group of teachers. Since I was not accustomed to speaking publicly for Christ, I asked how many teachers would be there. Fred's "Oh, about two hundred" caused my knees to buckle, but I went down and shared what Christ meant to me.

For the most part, my first six months as a Christian were confined to eliminating preconceived ideas. My biggest hang-up was bitterness about my mother's death.

On Wednesday evenings, we met in different homes to study the Bible. Each evening, we closed in conversational prayer. I never prayed during these times and usually was irritated because people prayed about things I considered insignificant compared to the prayers I had offered for my mother's health.

Susie encouraged me to pray at home with her, but I was not open to these suggestions either.

Our turn to host the Wednesday night Bible study came on a 53-degree-below-zero evening. Due to the weather, Bob Hoobgar, our pastor, his wife, Jan, and their two children were the only ones to attend. Everything went fine until prayer time. It would not be much of a prayer meeting, I thought, if I did not join Susie, Bob, and Jan. Far from being trivial, this was a big step for me. It was another proof that the key to faith is the first step.

As I stepped out in faith, God began to remove the bitterness I had about my mother's death. The climax came at a Wednesday evening Bible study in the pastor's home. Susie was ill, but I attended because the charter for the new church was to be established. The pastor began by sharing some thoughts about the Christian life, then he asked each person to give a testimony about his relationship with Christ and desire to join the church. I happened to be sitting to the pastor's right, and the people began speaking from the pastor's left.

I had determined I would not join the church, but God spoke with love through the preceding eleven people. I began to speak my thoughts as planned, but tears began rolling down my face and I could not speak. In a few moments, the resentment and bitterness about my mother were gone. Through the grace of God, I had new eyes to view her death. As the years have passed, I can understand the situation more clearly and can even thank Him for taking home with Him this dear one I loved so much.

I will never forget the pastor's wife asking when Sunday evening services were to begin. Sunday evening services! She must be kidding. This was pretty hard for me to understand. I was already going on Wednesday nights and two and one-half hours on Sunday mornings. Wasn't that enough? Besides, I had disciplined myself all through college, and now Sunday nights were TV nights for the Crowells. We always watched "The Wonderful World of Disneyland" and "Combat."

The church went ahead with evening services, and we still watched "The Wonderful World of Disneyland" and "Combat." However, we missed our friends at church and finally elected to give up TV.

We never missed a service the rest of the year. We loved the singing and sharing and thoroughly enjoyed seeing many people's lives, as well as our own, changed by the love of our Savior. My biggest encounter with practical experience occurred after I had resigned my position at the University of Alaska to accept a doctoral fellowship at the University of New Mexico. In the transition period, Susie and I vacationed in Coeur d'Alene, Idaho, a resort city and Susie's hometown. We had a grand time water skiing, swimming, and relaxing.

One evening the telephone rang. Fred Dyson was calling from Arrowhead Springs, California, to ask me to come there for three weeks to help organize a basketball team for Campus Crusade for Christ. "This will be a tremendous opportunity for you and Susie to study the Bible, enjoy Southern California, and meet some great Christians," Fred said.

I replied with, "Don't give me any of this three-week business, Dyson. I know you are trying to recruit me to come on full-time staff with Crusade for Christ." My reaction to this was identical to one some months earlier when I had discovered that people in the church were praying for me to go into full-time Christian service. I told these people to pray for other things, because nothing repulsed me more than the idea of becoming a missionary.

I told Fred I would pray about his invitation. Susie and I considered the matter seriously and consulted with Pastor Raymond Fitzhugh, the minister who had led Susie to Christ eleven months before.

I knew if I went, I wouldn't want to leave. After much thought, we decided to stay in Idaho. We would stop by Arrowhead Springs for a Leadership Training Institute later in the summer and then continue on to the University of New Mexico. I wrote Dyson a long letter loaded with apologies and mailed it airmail, special delivery. I thought this would get him off my back politely.

Several days later, Dyson called again to tell me that the team was in desperate straits with no organization or supervision. Would we come for just three weeks? I was puzzled because he sounded as though he had not received the letter which had clearly stated my intentions. For some reason, Susie and I both felt compelled to go to California, but I told Dyson not to feel hurt when I climbed on a plane in three weeks and left again.

We were excited as we flew out of Spokane International Airport. I had my tennis racquet, golf clubs, swimming trunks, and basketball gear. Most of all, I think we were just anxious to see our good friends the Dysons.

Fred and Jane met our plane in Ontario, California, and I immediately asked Dyson if he had received my letter. He had not received it and did not receive it for another month. We were convinced this was part of God's plan, because Fred would never have called if he had read my letter.

There were over a thousand people from all over the world at the conference. Since we had arrived a week late, accommodations on the grounds were unavailable and we had to stay in a motel. Everything seemed to be mass confusion with people roaming everywhere. I had expected to be with Dyson most of the time but saw him only two or three times during our entire stay at Arrowhead. We were so far behind in the institute of biblical studies program that we despaired of ever catching up. There certainly was no time for golf, tennis, or swimming. On top of this, a heat wave hit Arrowhead Springs with temperatures soaring to more than 108 degrees. Quite a change after a winter of subzero weather in Alaska. But as days passed and we became accustomed to our new surroundings, we were deeply impressed with the life pattern of those going through training.

A number of young men had already committed themselves to the basketball team. Mack Crenshaw, a big fellow who graduated from the University of Georgia where he was captain of the basketball team, really inspired me to make my life count for Christ. Larry Tregoning, captain of the Michigan team that placed second in the nation in 1965, and his wife, Ruth, were also a great influence. Never had Susie and I been around people whose style of living had so much to offer us.

Fortunately, when I was asked about the possibility of coaching the team, I had a perfect out. After all, we were already committed: Susie had a contract to teach the third grade, and I had to honor my contract with the University of New Mexico. I did not want to deal with the possibility of being released from these contracts without complication.

As the days passed, I was in tremendous turmoil. I knew I could go to New Mexico and still be a good Christian, but I realized I would not be very effective. I knew I was weak and the intense study for a doctorate would leave me little time to study the Bible. But the thought of becoming a missionary still turned me off. I just could not see myself doing this. Susie would say, "Let's pray about our decision." (I had a habit of procrastinating about tough decisions and letting time say no for me.) Susie was persistent, though, in wanting to settle it immediately. She wanted to stay—and pray that God would make us comfortable with that decision if it were right. I did not like that idea. I wanted to pray that we would go to New Mexico, and if God wanted us to stay He would make us miserable with that decision.

After much thought and prayer, we decided to call the dean of physical education at the University of New Mexico to find out if there would be a problem if I resigned my fellowship and teaching responsibilities. I will never forget that day as long as I live. I was more nervous than I had ever been in my life. Deep down I wanted him to solve everything by saying it just was not possible to change plans at this late date. On the other hand, even though I still wanted that doctoral degree, I felt a tremendous need to be with Campus Crusade. I knew this was what we should do. To make matters even worse, Larry Tregoning was standing across from the desk, praying as I made the call!

Without question, this was the toughest phone call I had ever made. Even talking to the operator was difficult. I hoped the dean would not be in his office. My hopes were in vain. Nervously, I explained that I had spent the past three weeks with Campus Crusade for Christ and as a result felt they had the answer to the serious problems facing America today. I told him I strongly desired to make my life count serving Jesus Christ, and yet I did not want to put him in a bind by asking to be relieved of my assignment.

The dean quickly assured me that I was not imposing because there were many to fill my place, and he certainly could not argue with my desire to serve Christ through Campus Crusade. He even stated that should I ever want to reapply, the door would be open.

Tregoning was jumping all over the room as I hung up the phone, and I just sat there stunned. I still had one out. Susie had a contract to honor. She immediately got the assistant superintendent of Albuquerque Public Schools on the telephone. After she explained the situation, he told her he was happy she called now because this was the last day the school district would release teachers from their contracts. Could God's leading be any more conclusive? Susie and I both knew we were on the correct road in spite of my bucking.

The evening before, we had gone out to dinner with Kent and Diane Hutcheson, who were serving Christ with Campus Crusade. That evening Kent shared with us some of the goals for his life and brought my attention to a Bible verse that gave me the necessary impetus to make the telephone call to Albuquerque.

The verse he quoted was, *"But we Christians have no veil over our faces; we can be mirrors that brightly reflect the glory of the Lord. And as the Spirit of the Lord works within us, we become more and more like Him."* **(2 CORINTHIANS 3:18 TLB)**.

Kent explained he wanted to become more Christ-like and take on His image as he went through life. I came to the conclusion this was the most important goal in life, and I began to ask God to make it real in my experience. Consequently, I knew it was essential to get myself involved in a situation where I could mature in Christ. Working with the dedicated men of the Athletes in Action basketball team was the best environment possible for me to grow spiritually.

Current Reflections

A brilliant professor made a statement I have never forgotten. He said, "Doctrine is dynamic, and revelation always demands a response." In simple terms, this means truth is explosive and knowledge demands action. In the basketball world, it means a team is much more effective doing three skills exceptionally well as opposed to doing thirty things poorly.

Our relationship with God is a two-way street. Over the years, it has become increasingly clear that love and obedience are the two ways on the street. This makes the relationship very practical! We demonstrate our love and obedience for Him by loving people. He does not command us to convert or to change people to our viewpoints or way of life. He merely makes it very simple by saying, "By this all men will know that you are My disciples, if you love one another" (JOHN 13:35). Because God first loved us, we are empowered to love Him and people.

During my early spiritually formative years, it became very clear to me that life is not a one-way street. Every action has a corresponding reaction. This is how my faith became practical. I realized my faith was not real faith unless it motivated me to action. God has taken, and often takes, the first step; therefore, it is always our move.

Chapter Notes

Chapter Notes

MEET **MY**
HEAD
COACH

4

GOD, I WANT TO BE PRACTICAL, BUT-

"

In the summer of 1974, a friend and I were riding in the back seat of his family's car from Moscow, Idaho, to northern California. As recent high school graduates, we had been selected to participate on a basketball team that would be traveling to Australia. My friend handed me a book to read to help pass the time on our long drive. This was my first introduction to Fred Crowell and his book *Meet My Head Coach*. It was a clear presentation of the Gospel of Jesus Christ and one man's story of how God drew him to Himself. Two years later, my former high school basketball coach asked me if I would like to work at a basketball camp for two weeks during the summer. I jumped at the opportunity since I had been studying sports medicine at Washington State University, and there was a need for an athletic trainer at the camp. I had not made the connection that the man who had written *Meet My Head Coach* was also the man who owned that basketball camp.

This was the beginning of one of the most significant relationships in my life. God used Fred Crowell to help me overcome some physical deformities I have had since birth. Fred was very encouraging and supportive as I learned to deal with my handicap. I have also benefited tremendously from the gifts of leadership God has given Fred. He has an innate understanding of how to train children, not only in basketball skills, but also in applying godly principles to their lives. Fred was gracious to offer me a full-time position with NBC Camps.

Twelve years later, God called me from NBC Camps to be the principal of a new classical and Christian school. It became apparent that God had been using NBC Camps and Fred Crowell to prepare me for this position. Classical Christian education has an old and well-tested pedagogy that is not unknown to the teaching tools of NBC Camps. Children, between the ages of five and twelve, profit from repetition and concrete direction. Fred Crowell is not unfamiliar with this type of teaching methodology. His camps repeatedly drill the fundamentals of basketball, serving as a strong foundation for the development of higher-level skills.

I am thankful for where God has led me, but probably even more thankful for the wisdom and change God has brought about in my life from my relationship with Fred Crowell.

BRUCE L. WILLIAMS

BRUCE WILLIAMS LIVES IN SPOKANE, WASHINGTON, WITH HIS WIFE, SUSAN. HE HAS TWO CHILDREN: LEAH, A SOPHOMORE IN COLLEGE, AND TAL, A FRESHMAN IN HIGH SCHOOL. WHILE ATTENDING WASHINGTON STATE UNIVERSITY AS A COLLEGE STUDENT, BRUCE BEGAN WORKING WITH NBC CAMPS. HE IS FOUNDER AND THE EXISTING PRINCIPAL OF THE OAKS CLASSICAL CHRISTIAN ACADEMY IN SPOKANE.

Flying at 33,000 feet, high above the beautiful Sierra, I slowly began to realize the serious dilemma I would be facing in a few short hours. My stomach tightened and beads of perspiration formed on my forehead, as I thought about the ominous responsibility of explaining to Susie's parents our decision to join Campus Crusade for Christ.

I mean, really, how does one explain to his family the logic of going from an annual income of over $18,000 to a salary of $350 a month? However, the rub was not the huge drop in salary but the way we would receive our salary on the staff of Campus Crusade. Each staff member, before reporting to his assignment, must ask individuals and groups to support his personal ministry. If the money is not raised, no salary is given.

This did not seem much of an obstacle, as we had talked at Arrowhead Springs with others who had previously raised their support. In fact, we gave it very little thought because everything was going so well and everyone was so enthusiastic. But our confidence slipped as we sat on the jetliner thinking about the next six weeks. It was a good thing I had burned the bridges to New Mexico or I might have missed out on one of the greatest blessings of my life.

Susie's folks met us at the airport and were full of questions. They knew very little about Campus Crusade for Christ. Susie's father was a successful businessman who had the ability to ask just the right questions. We were not eager to talk about the salary structure of our new position. The pension plan, insurance, and extra benefits were nothing to shout about. Later in the evening, Susie and I had a conference in our room and decided we must present the entire story to her parents. Our strategy was simple. Susie would tell her folks, and I would go to bed and pray for her!

My brave, little wife went into the living room and told her folks the entire financial picture of Campus Crusade. I won't go so far as to say my in-laws agreed with our decision, but they certainly were gracious about it. More than anything they wanted us to be happy. If this was what was going to make us happy, they were in favor of our joining Campus Crusade for Christ. Their attitude encouraged both of us.

Have you ever gone to someone to ask for money for your personal use? This was extremely difficult for me. I had come from a family where money was scarce. I had vowed I would be financially independent when I became an adult. I did not like thinking about it, but Susie gently kept telling me I needed to get out and talk to people about our support. One morning at the breakfast table, I was trying to muster up enough courage to begin making contacts when Susie's father asked, "When are you going out to start begging?" I nearly choked, but Susie shoved me out the door and said, "You can do it, honey."

I had a long list of contacts. Thinking myself a shrewd businessman, I decided to see one of my prime prospects. I had been told that this man would be happy to invest in my ministry. Before entering the man's store, I asked the Lord to help me present my program. I spotted the owner immediately and asked if I could take a few minutes to share with him my involvement with Campus Crusade for Christ. "I'm a businessman, and I don't have time to talk with you," was his gruff response, and off he stomped. It did not take me long to get back in the car! As I sat behind the steering wheel, God changed my attitude from hostility to peace, even compassion, for this man. I thanked God for this experience which helped me realize I was working for God, not to earn the favor of men. My responsibility was to control my actions so that Christ would be glorified. I began to give this awesome support-raising challenge to God.

Shortly after this experience, I was following up leads in Spokane. Someone had given me Charles Parsons' name. As I shared my plans with him and told my story, I noticed tears welling up in his eyes. I could hardly believe my ears when he said, "I count it a privilege to share in your wonderful work." I attempted to show my deep appreciation, but Mr. Parsons stopped me.

"Please don't thank me. This is my privilege, and I should be thanking you." God provided the encouragement I needed at exactly the right time. Charlie and Dorothy Parsons have been faithful friends, always encouraging us when we needed it most.

God continued to show His love and demonstrate His desire for us to be practical with Him by sending us several businessmen to invest in our ministry. I began to have a new perspective on raising financial support.

Another source of encouragement came from the doctor who first challenged Susie to consider the claims of Jesus Christ. Dr. Jane adopted us as her spiritual children. I preached my first sermon (on witnessing!) at St. Paul Memorial, the church where Susie met Christ the previous year. The love and encouragement we received here was overwhelming.

It was absolutely essential that we raised our support within six weeks, because we had to get ready for the basketball season. Since each game was under contract, and there was no postponement of dates, it was important that we use our time wisely. I averaged eleven speaking engagements a week. Against my better judgment, I accepted a speaking engagement in a farming community a number of miles away from Coeur d'Alene. Counting ourselves and the pastor, there were only nine people there. Of course we were very disappointed, because it was obvious this church was not in a position to take on new responsibilities. About the time we were feeling sorry for ourselves because of the poor turnout, a man stood and asked permission to read a letter from his son serving in Vietnam. According to the father, his son had always been closed to spiritual things. Great joy flooded the room as the father read of his son's decision to follow Christ. The letter went on to say the entire platoon had come to Christ, with only one exception, through the ministry of the son. Again our heavenly Father had taught us an important lesson. Even though we did not receive financial support, our hearts were lifted, and we were thankful for the prayer support.

Since I am sharing learning situations, the following is a lesson Susie learned during our support-raising experiences in Idaho. When Susie received Christ, one of the questions she wanted answered before making a decision concerned her responsibility to tell others. Because so many people had approached us about religion, we were dead set against talking to others about it. The pastor assured Susie she would never have to tell others until she desired to do so. Now, one year later, Susie had the privilege of sharing the claims of Christ with her sister. Patti listened attentively and immediately decided she wanted Christ as her Savior and Lord. Susie could hardly contain herself as she told me about it later in the evening.

As we prepared to raise support in my hometown, all my apprehension and fear returned. When I had given my life to basketball, practicing over two hundred days a year, everyone thought me admirable; but now that I gave my life and time to Jesus Christ, I would be considered odd. I did not want to be branded a religious fanatic. More than anything I wanted my family and friends to discover Jesus Christ was for real.

What could I expect them to think? Since I had not been home much for several years, the change was more obvious to my friends. One of the biggest critics of religion had gone off to Alaska and come back filled with it. They thought I had taken a 180-degree turn and really did not know how to react. One of my closest friends considered wearing his shirt backward in my presence. Other close friends debated whether to invite us to their home. One of our medical bills was forwarded to us while we spent a few days in one home, and they were glad to see we still believed in doctors. Time and again we were told, "It is fine to have a religion, but don't go overboard."

I was a living example of GALATIANS 6:7 TLB which reminds us that "...a man will always reap just the kind of crop he sows!" For years I had made it clear that religion was a bunch of baloney and the church was filled with hypocrites. Consequently, I was unable to convince some of my friends that I could not go halfway with Christ, because He was the most meaningful experience in my life. Jesus Christ said, "You will know the truth, and the truth will set you free" (JOHN 8:32). I had been set free by the power of His love; my bitterness and critical attitude toward religion had vanished. I had come to grips with ROMANS 5:8 TLB, "But God showed His great love for us by sending Christ to die for us while we were still sinners." That meant me! There just was no possible way I could go halfway with Him.

However as the days passed, family and friends saw we were still normal and had all our faculties. As they saw our deep convictions and a lifestyle they could respect, they began to ask serious questions about Christ. Before we left for our assignment at Arrowhead Springs, many in my family received Christ as their Savior. Since then many of my closest friends, who were very skeptical, have met Jesus Christ. Susie and I were overjoyed to see the power of God's love. It was difficult to raise support in my hometown, but God gave us something better.

We did not know for sure if the necessary funds had been raised, but it was essential for us to leave for California to begin our new assignment. Though we were anxious to get settled in an apartment, our first stop when we arrived in San Bernardino was the accounting department at Arrowhead Springs to find out how successful our past six weeks had been. We had received no paycheck the entire summer and were hoping one would be waiting for us. If the money was in our account, we were entitled to receive checks for August and September.

We were very optimistic, because we had talked to many people and averaged over ten speaking engagements each week. We were determined to raise enough so we could give our full attention to our ministry. As we went to the accounting office, Susie and I speculated excitedly about the amount of money in our account. I remember telling Susie I would be happy if we had $1,000.

What a surprise we had in store for us. The lady at the desk solemnly told us there were not sufficient funds for us to receive any money. In fact, we were fifty dollars in the red!

God did not let this experience go to waste, however. He taught us something that has stood us in good stead ever since and initiated a practice that has become an integral part of our marriage. The Scripture says, *"Let us consider how to stimulate one another to love and good deeds"* (HEBREWS 10:24 NASB). When I walked out of the accounting office, I was ready to throw in the towel, but Susie was extremely optimistic and began to encourage me. There has never been a time since when both of us were discouraged at once, regardless of circumstances. In each calamity one of us has been able to apply God's promise of stimulating one another to love and good deeds. We have been grateful for this lesson in patience, because Susie and I firmly believe we can conquer any problem providing we work together to solve the difficulty by applying biblical principles.

Christianity became almost uncomfortably practical when it came to trusting God for money. The previous year Uncle Sam had taken more out of our monthly checks than we were presently earning. I don't know what others on staff do when they don't get a check, but I do know it was not pleasant for the Crowells. We soon learned Campus Crusade's financial philosophy helped create total dependence upon God to supply our needs. Paydays are exciting times because they give us an opportunity to trust God that, unfortunately, most Americans, receiving their salaries month after month, never have. Many of the most exciting times I have had are the result of God meeting financial need. God has proven time and again the reality of Paul's claim in PHILLIPIANS 4:19, *"And my God will meet all your needs according to His glorious riches in Christ Jesus."*

Learning this principle of God's sufficiency has not been easy. One difficult experience occurred at the end of our first basketball season with Athletes in Action. Our finances were so bad we were forced to take a month off to raise money. We had an exceptional ministry in people's lives during this month. It appeared we had done very well in raising funds; however, when we returned to California, we discovered we were in debt to the tune of $350.

To be perfectly honest, I was bewildered. I prayed, "Lord, I will never again ask another person for support unless You specifically direct me. I ask You for a ministry in people's lives, and I will leave the money raising up to You. When the money does not come in, I will know one of two things: I am not having a ministry and better get busy, or You want me in some other work. Thank You, Lord. Amen." Then I left the house for a summer game. As I left Susie said, "Honey, it is going to take a miracle to get us out of the red." A miracle happened two hours later. John Pittman phoned from Birmingham, Alabama to inform us that he had mailed $300 to our account.

The next time we traveled to share experiences with our friends, we did not mention finances even though our account had a deficit of $150. When asked, we said God was supplying our needs. We spoke at a Sunday service in Spokane, and to our surprise the pastor called for a love offering. No one had ever done this before, and no one here knew our need. When the offering was counted it was $150!

How exciting it is to trust God, to take all our needs directly to Him and not to men. God has proved faithful by moving men without any word from us. This philosophy is easy when you have no financial problems. It is almost impossible to practice when money gets tight. Our first response is to send out an SOS, "We need $500 for the doctor bill." This is the logical approach but, in our case, not God's method.

One morning Susie felt constrained to ask the Lord for fourteen dollars to take some non-Christian ladies to Christian Women's Club to hear an outstanding speaker. In the mail early that afternoon she received an envelope with no return address. The only thing enclosed was a ten-dollar bill and a five-dollar bill.

These examples could go on ad infinitum. Each day is an adventure as we trust God for the impossible. Our God can and will supply all our needs if we only ask Him. He eagerly waits to prove His promise: "*Now glory be to God who by His mighty power at work within us is able to do far more than we would ever dare to ask or even dream of*" (EPHESIANS 3:20 TLB).

Can you name something specific God has done this past week for you or your family? If you want to begin a practical walk with Christ, I encourage you to begin now by being as specific and down-to-earth as possible in the things you ask of God.

Project 2

- Look up the following verses in your Bible:

  John 15:6

  Jeremiah 33:3

  Philippians 4:6-7

  Philippians 4:19

  I John 5:14-15

- Write down specific things God has done in your life.

- List specific things on paper that you would like to see God do. After you have made your list, begin to apply the principles set forth in the five Bible verses you just examined under Bullet #1 above.

Current Reflections

In a world that seems to revolve around money, not having any can be very trying. As a young coach, I quickly had an intuitive understanding of the importance of money. To then be put in the position of having to ask for financial assistance if I wanted an income, was a real test of faith, to put it mildly.

And yet, the world's most famous prayer, "Our Father who art in heaven... give us this day, our daily bread," speaks of daily provision for life, implying God works in the details of life. If God does not work in the day-to-day operation of my life, how will I be able to trust Him in my death?

In retrospect, that challenging time of trusting God to provide financially established a foundation for trusting God completely. I have learned that faith is the refusal to panic. It is also the way God has chosen to bless us, producing an inner peace that cannot be duplicated.

In reading this chapter as a 64-year-old looking back on my life, not as a 31-year-old looking forward, I have experienced the reality of God being faithful to be practical in every situation and life experience. Forty years is more than sufficient history for me to believe He will deliver on His promises, as I trust Him in the final years, the winter, of my life.

Chapter Notes

MEET **MY**
HEAD
COACH

5

TOO GOOD TO BE TRUE

"

In August of 1989, I flew from Greece to the state of Washington in order to attend NBC Camps. There I met Fred Crowell for the first time. The next two weeks had a great impact on me, and I still consider them two of the most important weeks of my whole life! During that time, Fred spoke both to my heart and my mind, motivating me to become a better person. His testimony affected me deeply!

Before returning home, Fred gave me a copy of his book *Meet My Head Coach*, which I read as soon as I arrived home in Greece. Needless to say, the book is powerful and spiritually challenging. Yet it is more than that. It is a personal, face-to-face meeting with the truth of Christ—that He lives, that He loves, and that He saves! I saw this in every word I read. Why should I not want to experience the reality of Jesus Christ? That is why *Meet My Head Coach* is still my favorite book: it motivated me to use my life to the maximum for God's glory.

There is one more reason why *Meet My Head Coach* is my favorite book. Fred has indicated the book would have been impossible without the young men who dedicated their lives to God and served Him through Athletes in Action. Both of us have history with AIA: Fred was its first basketball coach, and I had the privilege to be the first associate staff member of AIA in Italy.

I am proud to call Fred my brother and co-worker. Seventeen years later, I can still feel the joy he has in his faith, and I still apply the principles of living learned from him. The Lord is faithful to bless us as we seek Him!

TIMOS PHILIPPOU

BORN IN CYPRUS, TIMOS OBTAINED HIS DEGREE IN PHYSICAL THERAPY FROM THE UNIVERSITY OF ROME, ITALY, AND HAS LIVED IN ROME SINCE 1984. HE IS A STAFF MEMBER OF THE ITALIAN NATIONAL JUNIOR BASKETBALL TEAM AND THE PRESIDENT OF NBC CAMPS ITALIA. HE AND HIS WIFE, MARIA MARMARA, HAVE TWO CHILDREN, ALEXANDER AND LIDIA.

T IME-OUT!" I yelled. Ten thousand screaming fans were going wild, and the score was 23-5 against my team after five minutes of play. I had always dreamed of coaching in big time college athletics, but my dream certainly had not included being slaughtered.

Athletics in Action was losing its second game in major college competition. Tonight it was Wichita State; the previous evening we had been beaten by the University of Utah. We had won six consecutive games against small colleges, but now we were playing the best universities in America.

I knew we were in for a rough night of basketball because Wichita State had a fine basketball team, and we were exhausted from an all-day flight that had begun at six o'clock in the morning. To further complicate things, after arriving in Wichita we had spent over two hours trying to find the homes we were to stay in. Normally the team stayed in private homes. It gave team members an opportunity to influence many young people and helped us meet expenses. However, the late hours did not contribute favorably to our performance on court.

I had little hope of victory as our men went back on court after the time-out—not when we were trailing by eighteen points after only five minutes of play. Miraculously, we began to click and played sensational basketball in the next fifteen minutes, leading Wichita 46-44 at half-time. The fans were in a frenzy. Half-time is valuable for teams to rest and prepare strategy for the second half, but for Athletes in Action half-time is strategic for another reason. During this fifteen-minute half-time period, the good news of Jesus Christ is presented to the audience by the players on the team.

When we started, we did not know if we would be accepted or booed. Since every player shared this apprehension, we became a very close unit. We grew closer to each other than any team I had ever associated with because Jesus Christ was our unifying force. Basketball was our chance to communicate "the most joyful news ever announced, and it is for everyone!" (LUKE 2:10 TLB). Each of us was aware of the awesome responsibility for making our play consistent with what we said at half-time.

Immediately at the half-time buzzer of this Wichita game, we formed a line at the free throw line while one of our players carried the microphone onto the court. We were nervous but encouraged to see that nearly every spectator remained in his seat for our presentation.

Ricky Mill, a 6'7" forward from the University of Georgia, began. "Ladies and gentlemen, it is a privilege for Athletes in Action to be here tonight to play Wichita State University. Athletes in Action is a division of Campus Crusade for Christ. We are here tonight not only because we love to play basketball, but, more importantly, because we desire to have a positive impact on America. We believe we must change our society, but in order to change society, we must change individual lives. Education, legislation, and social causes are all good, but they don't change the basic nature of man. We have found in our experience that the only person who can effectively change an individual is Jesus Christ. Now I would like a couple of my teammates to tell you how Jesus Christ changed their lives."

While Ricky was speaking, one of the announcers giving game statistics overheard him. Abruptly he said to his radio audience, "Wait a minute. These guys are talking about Christ. You have to hear what they are saying." Immediately, he brought his microphone out onto the floor to pick up our presentation.

I do not remember who did give testimonies after Ricky spoke, but I would like you to read a couple from men who have a real impact for Christ.

The first testimony is Clint Hooper's. Clint is very effective sharing his faith in one-to-one situations.

> I was very young when my father explained to me that church attendance in itself was not the way to God. Realizing that Christ was "the Way, the Truth and the Life" as He said, I prayed, receiving Him by faith. At that time, He brought me peace of mind and contentment in Him. He also gave me the answers to the big questions in life: Who am I? Where am I going? Why am I here?

> But there were still practical problems in our society to be faced. I was about eleven years old when I became painfully aware of the difference in skin pigmentation in this country. As I looked within the black community in which I lived and saw the strife and internal conflicts, even Christianity began to look like a religion of hypocrites!

Through college, I continued my search for answers to the black and white problems in America. Later, I discovered that following Jesus is the only permanent solution to any of man's problems. We, who are black, have one main desire: to be free to fulfill the destiny for which all men were created rather than have our destiny controlled by some outside group. The Bible clearly teaches that it is not God's will for any group to be oppressed by another but that real freedom is to be found only in knowing Jesus Christ.

Now, as a member of the Athletes in Action basketball team, I can share God's answer with all men—black, white, yellow, or red—because I know that all men, regardless of color, are in bondage without Christ in their lives.

The following testimony is given by Jeff Mackey. Jeff played with the team one year and has worked with Campus Crusade for Christ's high school ministry since then.

When I was in high school, I lived for three things: basketball, grades and my girl friend, but not necessarily in that order. When these areas of my life were going well, I was happy and content. But when they were not going well, I had no one but myself to blame, because I was in control of these areas.

Then something happened that I couldn't control. My parents separated and were later divorced. I felt very unloved and alone. I built a shell and never let myself get close to anyone. I felt that any success that I would have in life would have to be the result of my own efforts.

As I carried this independent attitude on to college, I set two goals for myself: I wanted to become the best basketball player I could, and I wanted to make good grades. However, I found college basketball more demanding than I had anticipated, and my goals were never realized. Even though I studied hard and did well academically, I found that all I had to look forward to was the next test and that my studying really didn't answer the questions I had about life and happiness.

In the spring of my freshman year, I met a man who told me how I could have a personal relationship with Jesus Christ by asking Him into my life as my Savior and Lord As I sat there thinking, I said to myself, "Jeff, you really haven't given this too much thought, but your life hasn't been going as well as you wanted it to go; if Christ can do all that He claimed for you, you've got everything to gain and nothing to lose by receiving Him."

As I began to meet with other students who had Christ in their lives, I began to feel wanted as a person instead of just a basketball player. My temper almost vanished, and I became more patient with others. For the first time in my life, I began to love my parents sincerely. I began learning how to live above my circumstances instead of letting them control me. And even though I've done a lot of different things and had a lot of fun in college, I realized that my most meaningful and rewarding experiences were directly related to learning about Christ's love and watching others respond to Him.

We received an excellent round of applause as we concluded and began to prepare for the second half of play. Wichita State came out in a full-court press, and we lost a hard-fought 97-89 game in the last minute of play.

As the game ended, we immediately took our place at the free throw line to present the remainder of our program. Two more players gave their personal testimonies before the captain of our team, Mack Crenshaw came to the microphone to explain how one could come into a personal relationship with Jesus Christ.

I was upset as I walked onto the floor, disgusted about the loss, blaming the referees. I felt I was learning more about the devil every day. He wore a black-and-white striped shirt and blew a whistle! Standing there, lamenting the lost game, I heard Mack ask anyone interested in receiving information about how to mature in his relationship with Christ to turn to the back page in the program. Thousands of people responded. God was showing me that winning the basketball game was insignificant compared to our ultimate purpose.

God, in His wonderful ways, has seen fit to move the hearts of men across our nation to make it possible for us to play basketball for His glory and honor. Only nine months before this Wichita game, Athletes in Action was only a dream. Dave Hannah, the director of Athletes in Action, was told it would take four or five years to get it off the ground. However, Hannah was aggressive and got approval from the National Association of Collegiate athletics to schedule games against college teams. Then he got both Larry Tregoning and Mack

Crenshaw, then on the staff with Campus Crusade for Christ, to agree to play on the team, provided a suitable basketball schedule could be arranged. No amateur college grad team in America was having success scheduling games with college teams, but within three days, while Dave, Mack, and Larry were at the NCAA basketball finals in Louisville, Kentucky, over forty different universities indicated interest in scheduling Athletes in Action. Before the spring of 1967, such outstanding universities as California, Stanford, Florida State, Colorado State, Toledo, Tulsa, Wichita State, Oregon, and Oregon State were lined up for games. The most remarkable thing was that not one athletic director or coach asked who coached the team or who was going to play on it. Fortunate also, because thus far, Hannah had only two players and not even a coach!

Only nine months earlier, I had invited Jesus Christ into my life, asking to experience Him in practical ways in my coaching, teaching, family life, and relationships with other people. Now I had the privilege of coaching a basketball team whose primary purpose was to communicate the love of Jesus Christ—a basketball team that hadn't even existed nine months before.

The response to our team exceeded our wildest imaginations. At each of our games, we collected comment cards which helped us gauge audience response to our program. These comment cards were an encouragement to us, too. Here are some of the comments we received from various games:

> A school principal: "I've never witnessed anything quite like this demonstration. It's wonderful to know that our world isn't completely lost."

> A 12-year-old: "It was beautiful the way you did it. It meant a lot to me and others. The game was good, too!"

> A student: "I found a start tonight. I would like to follow it up in Christ."

> A 36-year-old university professor: "Very glad you came. Peace and joy. Thanks for the straight stuff."

> An 18-year-old car wash attendant: "You pinned me down to a dime because I'm very lonely, depressed, and all those other things. I would

like to know if there is anything for not-too-good of an athlete like me."

A 17-year-old athlete: "I would like to thank you for coming to Peoria and showing me that I really do need Jesus Christ."

A mother: "I am really impressed with what you men have said here tonight. It makes me realize that we, as parents, have neglected this area of our children's lives."

A youth: "I am twelve years old. What can I do to help?"

Opposing coaches responded favorably to the team's witness and play on court, too. Jerry Tarkanian, then basketball coach for Cal State, Long Beach, California, said, "In this day and age of unrest, it gives us a great deal of pride to see a group of young men who are dedicated to Christianity and the principles of our country. The dedication and sacrifice of your group are a pleasure to behold." Russell M. Walseth, head basketball coach of the University of Colorado at Boulder wrote, "Their oneness and unity in following Christ certainly showed up in their excellent team play and determination on the court."

Our desire was to demonstrate the reality of Jesus Christ and to challenge people to be practical in everyday living situations with Him. God has honored that desire and in addition to giving the team favor, gave them the opportunity of seeing people changed. There were many examples of transformed lives. Let me tell you about one.

One day in November, 1967, Steve Read decided to attend a church. He had been an alcoholic for ten years. It was not that Steve enjoyed his life as an alcoholic. He had gone through nearly every treatment for alcoholism without success. Finally in desperation, he decided to give God a chance, and if this failed, he would end his life.

The apostle Paul, in his letter to the Corinthian church, explains that God has a solution for every problem. *"But remember this—the wrong desires that come into your life aren't anything new and different. Many others have faced exactly the same problems before you. And no temptation is irresistible. You can trust God to keep the temptation from becoming so strong that you can't stand up against it, for He promised this and will do what He says. He will show you how to escape temptation's power so that you can bear up patiently against it"* (1 CORINTHIANS 10:13 TLB). Steve was no exception. Standing in the foyer of a church one Sunday, he met Ray Burwick. Ray was a college basketball coach who, until this time, had never seen God change anyone's life except his own. He was very concerned when Steve stated he was going to give God a try, but if He failed, suicide was all that was left. Quietly, but firmly, Ray shared God's love and asked Steve to telephone him if he ever needed help.

The following day Steve called, asking Ray for the promised help. That was the day Steve asked Jesus Christ to be his Lord and Savior. Slowly but surely, God began to work a miracle in his life. It was not an easy process, and Ray found himself spending many hours each day praying and studying the Bible with Steve, asking God to make it possible for Steve to succeed.

Four months following Steve's decision for Christ, our basketball team came to town. Since Ray was a basketball devotee, he asked Steve to be his guest at the game, but Steve disliked basketball and thought it was ridiculous for a group of athletes to talk about Christ at a basketball game. After much persuasion, Steve finally agreed to attend.

Several months later, I had the privilege of meeting Steve, and he confessed that "the silly old basketball game" proved to be the turning point in his life. "It was the greatest night of my life. The fact that those young men were willing to stand before so many people and talk about Jesus Christ really moved me. I will never forget it as long as I live."

The most important thing about this story is that it is not over yet. Steve is still growing in his relationship with Christ and having a significant ministry in many other lives around him. And Ray Burwick can no longer say he has never seen God change anyone's life. In the process of seeing Steve's life changed, Ray also experienced the hand of God—he joined the team as an assistant basketball coach! Here is his remarkable testimony.

> "If I died for you, can't you stutter for me?" This was the question Christ posed to me in response to a very bitter attitude on my part. This attitude came to a climax one night as I was trying to share my faith in God with a group of people. I was stuttering so badly the people nearest me were getting a free shower. I vehemently told God that was the last time I would be speaking for Him.
>
> Fifteen years previously I had asked Christ to control my life, and He had guided me in some miraculous ways. But this stuttering bit had me defeated. It wasn't until I faced my circumstances that I realized how

insignificant was my pain and embarrassment in comparison to what Christ had gone through for me.

I saw then that He wanted to use me, imperfect as I was, to be a tool for Him. Now it is the greatest thrill in the world to share the claims of Jesus Christ across America, and to see people respond, to see them invite Christ into their lives of frustration and dissatisfaction to ones of peace, purpose and power. Christ said in JOHN 10:10 NASB, "I came that they might have life, and might have it abundantly."

This brings us right back to practical Christianity. Before our team had played its first game, we were primarily concerned about three areas. Realizing we had tackled a difficult schedule, we did not know if we could compete respectably. We were also concerned about the acceptance of our message, and finally, we were concerned about our ability to stand up under the pressures of the games, numerous speaking engagements, and excessive travel with little rest. In one season, Athletes in Action played forty-nine games, flew over 35,000 miles, and presented hundreds of programs. During this season, the team played twenty games in twenty-six days and traveled over 15,000 miles throughout Panama, Peru, Chili, Brazil, Ecuador, and Colombia.

God was more than faithful in all three areas of our concern. He made it possible for us to compete successfully against the best college teams in America. We played against and defeated such outstanding teams as Oregon, Washington, Southern Cal, Brigham Young, Bradley, and Kansas State. One year, we played ten of the top twenty ranked teams in the country. He gave us marvelous acceptance and met our personal needs as well.

We had many opportunities to test our faith while playing basketball. It was exciting to see the ways God used to bring us into a deeper walk with Him. Due to these experiences, I am committed to encourage everyone to be as practical as possible with God in every area of his life.

When we recruited new players for our team, we made a point of carefully explaining that this venture with Athletes in Action would be the most practical experience of their lives. Among ourselves, the team members often joked about being on the stretch rack. This was our definition of being in a position where the Lord could teach us to grow. When you are on the rack, you either grow in maturity or fold. King Solomon writes, "You are a poor specimen if you can't stand the pressure of adversity" (PROVERBS 24:10 TLB).

My purpose in sharing these experiences with you is not to place Athletes in Action on a pedestal as the epitome of Christian living, but to bring glory to Jesus Christ since He has made all this possible. Only when we have completely yielded to Him have we seen great results. People have been reached through the team for one reason alone: the reality of the love of Christ and His power to transform lives.

In GALATIANS 5:16-23, the apostle Paul compares two types of lives. First he describes the man who acts independently of God and whose life, as a result, is subject to conflict and turmoil. Then he describes the man who is controlled by the Holy Spirit, whose life is characterized by love, joy, peace, patience, kindness, faith, meekness, and self-discipline. He calls these qualities the "fruit" of the Holy Spirit. A big, juicy apple is the product of a healthy apple tree; qualities of love, joy, and peace are the products of a healthy relationship with Christ.

In the remaining chapters of this book, I have endeavored to offer practical, everyday solutions for a healthy walk with Jesus, using principles of Scripture, illustrated by the lives and experiences of people who have learned to be practical with their Creator.

Current Reflections

"Announcing peace, proclaiming news of happiness, good news, good news: our God reigns" is one of my favorite songs. I suppose it is partly because I delight in good news. I intensely dislike bad news, so much so, that I am a "bad news first" boy. My attitude is let's get the pain over now!

However, in reflecting back thirty-three years, I realize bad news has not devastated me. Maybe it is because any bad news is like a pebble. If I hold it too close to my eyes, it puts everything out of focus. Yet if I hold it at proper viewing distance, it can be examined and categorized. Best still, if I throw it down to the ground by my feet (in its truest setting), I can continue walking and it becomes only one tiny bump on my pathway.

In 1966, when I made the wonderful discovery of knowing Jesus Christ, even in writing "Meet My Head Coach" in 1973, I could not possibly have fathomed just how wonderful this discovery was going to be. Over two thousand years before, St. Paul wrote in Romans, "He who believes in Him will not be disappointed" (ROMANS 9:33 TLB). *That meant I could follow Him to the ends of the earth and not be let down. In all these years, I cannot think of one person who has told me they were disappointed following Christ as a head coach. On the other hand, when I think of any other leader who might make such a claim, I have to wonder, could I follow him to the ends of the earth and not be disappointed?*

My experience says St. Paul's quote in the first century remains true in this twenty-first century. You can bank on it. It is too good to be true!

Chapter Notes

Chapter Notes

MEET **MY**
HEAD
COACH

6

THE NAME OF THE GAME

"

St. Francis said, "Preach the gospel at all times; if necessary, use words." One of the most difficult aspects of life is to walk the talk. *Meet My Head Coach* is a story about how my father became a believer in Christ. It is the message of someone who experienced a radical change. To me, the most beautiful part of the message is that the Crowell family continues experiencing profound change, even thirty years after this book was originally written. My dad has made his relationship with Christ the foundation and center of his life. It is something that is practical and real for him and, through his example as well as my mother's, something that is real for our whole family on a daily basis.

Often, people say they wish they could win the lottery because their lives would be so much better. Yet research shows those who win the lottery are no happier a few years after winning than before they won. I feel like I've won a much greater and more amazing lottery, and my life will never be the same because of it. When my mom began a relationship with Christ, little did she know this relationship would change the whole course of our family history. Instead of continuing a generational pattern of distance, guilt and discontentment, she has given me the gift of joy and hope. My dad told me every day he loved me, asked me to forgive him when he hurt my feelings, and broke the cycle of abuse, neglect, rage and shame—all because of Christ.

I think about the vows Dad made to himself when his mom died: never cry again and never pray again. I find these are parallel to what Victor Hugo says about the human spirit, *"Dry eyes are the sign of a dead soul."* What I love about my dad is that Christ has made him alive. Because of the changes God has made in my mom and dad, I have a dad who cried on my wedding day and who prayed when my three children came into the world. I also have the privilege of a relationship with a father I admire and love.

JENNIFER S. FERCH

JENNIFER FERCH LIVES IN SPOKANE, WASHINGTON, WITH HER HUSBAND SHANN AND THREE BEAUTIFUL DAUGHTERS: NATALYA ALEXIS, ARIANA ALEXIS, AND ISABELLA ALEXIS. SHE IS A GRADUATE FROM BIOLA UNIVERSITY IN VOCAL PERFORMANCE AND HAS A MASTER'S DEGREE IN COUNSELING PSYCHOLOGY FROM GONZAGA UNIVERSITY. AT THE PRESENT, JENNIFER IS A VICE PRESIDENT AND WEB MASTER WITH NBC CAMPS, AUTHORING MANY OF ITS SUCCESSFUL PUBLICATIONS.

"

Fred Crowell's deep love for all good things has given him a gift for working with people of all ages. I remember listening to one of his speeches as a young, middle-school student. Fred presented the following profound notion: "As you speak, so you become." I was embittered against my own father. I often spoke darkly of him; if not openly, then in my heart. After hearing Fred, I was so impressed by the ideas he presented that I personally was moved to take action. The next time I approached my father, I embraced him and told him I loved him. My father received the embrace, and this moment became the turning point toward overcoming our differences and developing now many years of quality relationship.

I have Fred to thank, not only for encouraging me toward a more meaningful way of life, but for presenting time-honored truths grounded in the hope of a loving God. These truths, I believe, are foundational to the sacrifice and self-discipline involved in the pursuit of legitimate love in the contemporary world. Fred's approach to God and people reveals the beauty, subtlety, and legitimate power found in servanthood of Christ.

Because of the sheer grace of my contact with Fred, a desire to love and serve has come to enliven and set fire to everything in my life: from marriage and family, to art and science; from friendship and sports, to the daily gratitude that accompanies a life lived not merely to be loved but to love. Because of Fred's influence in my life, I have become a better man. I love my mom. I love my dad. I love my brother.

From this place, I have been granted not just the opportunity but the integrity to create a haven of strength and hope for my three young daughters, Natalya, Ariana and Isabella. These three cherished girls ("stars in the sky of God" I like to call them) are growing up in the peace and light I've always found in their mother. And she is great not only because God has created her to be so, but also because she has a great father and mother. Her father is Fred Crowell; her mother is Susie Crowell. Being in their presence has made all the difference. So now I can look into Jennifer's eyes, and into the eyes of our daughters, and say with confidence the beautiful words of Isaiah: *"God has given you the garment of praise instead of the spirit of despair."* Thank you, Fred, for helping us all weave a garment of praise!

DR. SHANN R. FERCH

DR. SHANN FERCH MAKES HIS HOME IN SPOKANE WITH HIS WIFE, JENNIFER, AND THREE REMARKABLE GIRLS. SHANN IS A FULL PROFESSOR AT GONZAGA UNIVERSITY IN THE DOCTORAL PROGRAM FOR LEADERSHIP STUDIES. HE IS A RECOGNIZED LEADER IN THE SERVANT-LEADERSHIP FIELD WITH SPECIALIZATION IN SOCIAL JUSTICE AND FORGIVENESS. SHANN GRADUATED FROM PEPPERDINE UNIVERSITY AS THE OUTSTANDING SENIOR MALE STUDENT, WITH A DEGREE IN ORGANIZATIONAL COMMUNICATIONS AND A MASTER'S DEGREE IN CLINICAL PSYCHOLOGY; HE RECEIVED HIS DOCTOR'S DEGREE FROM THE UNIVERSITY OF ALBERTA IN CANADA.

S atan doesn't care if every man on your team is a Christian, if he can prevent your being united," wrote Dr. Gene Davis, a veterinarian who prayed for us regularly. He had been instrumental in helping us in Portland, Oregon, during our first year of competition, with 300 people becoming Christians through the team's witnessing. Since then, he had prayed for us regularly. As Dr. Davis prayed for us, God revealed this important principle to him. Every Christian knows that Satan is continually trying to thwart his efforts to live the Christian life, but I did not fully comprehend Dr. Davis' statement.

He suggested in his letter that we read the seventeenth chapter of John's gospel. This chapter is the one that records Jesus' prayer just before His crucifixion. I was eager to know what He would pray for at this critical hour.

"I pray for them. I am not praying for the world, but for those You have given Me, for they are Yours. All I have Is Yours, and all You have Is Mine. And glory has come to Me through them. I will remain in the world no longer, but they are still in the world, and I am coming to You. Holy Father, protect them by the power of Your name--the name You gave Me--so that they may be one as we are one" (JOHN 17:9-11).

Jesus prayed that those His Father had given Him, (His disciples) would be as completely united as He and His Father were. Then in verses 20-23, I understood the logic of Dr. Davis' letter. Jesus prayed:

"My prayer is not for them alone. I pray also for those who will believe in Me through their message, that all of them may be one, Father, just as You are in Me and I am in You. May they also be in us so that the world may believe that You have sent Me. I have given them the glory that You gave Me, that they may be one as we are one: I in them and You in Me. May they be brought to complete unity to let the world know that You sent Me and have loved them even as You have loved Me" (JOHN 17:20-23).

It was obvious Jesus wanted to use the unity of believers in establishing the credibility of His claims to the world. Jesus prayed that His followers may be one in order that others would believe that God had sent Him. I do not believe anyone realizes the importance of unity more than a coach. Many teams have not been successful because they failed to cooperate as a unit. On the other hand, many teams with inferior talent have achieved success because every player was committed to team unity.

I began to meditate on unity among Christians. Since unity is essential any time two or more are involved, it applies to every situation—family, business, church, team. I saw that Satan has done an excellent job of dividing Christians. Many people feel that to belong to a denomination is to be a Christian. The family unit is constantly being attacked, and many question the need for the marriage ceremony. Two in five marriages in America will end in the divorce court. Yes, Scripture talks about Satan being the great divider, and he is doing his job well.

Although Satan knew that all of us on the team were Christians, he also knew our ministry could be greatly hindered if we were divided.

Ray Burwick, whose life had been challenged and changed in that first visit to Portland, which had also given us Dr. Davis to pray for our ministry, was now our assistant coach. As Ray and I prayed and discussed this chapter in John, we began to experience the Spirit of God teaching us. We were ripe for His message, because we had just suffered our worst defeat since forming the team. We had not played as a unit, and our players were discouraged.

To make this concept of unity even more practical, the results of lack of unity were clear in the family Ray and I were staying with. The line of communication between husband and wife had broken down, and the children were being affected. The team's poor showing, plus this situation, helped us realize the full import of Christ's prayer.

Ray and I, with the team, began to pray that we might function as a unit, reflecting the reality of Christ through our lives. Rather than to pray for many to receive Christ or for us to win a game, we simply asked the Lord to make it possible for the spectators to see the reality of Christ through our unity.

The following night, we played the University of Utah, which had an exceptionally good basketball team. It was obvious to all of us that God had answered prayer because of the oneness we demonstrated on the basketball court. We were not only hustling, but we were passing the ball to the open man and helping each other on defense. We lost the game by six points in the last few minutes of play, but we knew many had seen the reality of Christ. One university student doing graduate work in history told me after the game that he had never seen the love of God so real before.

In a matter of only a few days, we witnessed love and unity spring up within the family we were visiting too. It was heartwarming to hear the father and mother praying together. The wife began to show renewed interest in her duties as a housekeeper. The husband manifested consideration not previously demonstrated, improving his manners and re-establishing communication. The changes were obvious to everyone, especially the children.

Even though the team had a good ministry before receiving Dr. Davis' letter, we began to experience greater results by asking God for team unity. We wanted people to see Christ in us. Not only did we see more people receive Christ as their Savior, but we began to win more basketball games.

Shortly after this, we played Bradley University. Bradley had not lost a non-conference game in fifty-seven contests. A group of young people who had come to the game agreed to stay to hear our presentation if Athletes in Action won. This was a safe bet for them, in light of Bradley's home court record. One of our players threw in a spectacular shot with two seconds remaining in the game, and we won by two points. One of the boys in the group received Christ. His family is convinced that God answered their prayer for us to win the game. It was exciting to see specific answers to prayer.

As you read this chapter, do not procrastinate. Do not say that this does not apply to your situation. People all over the world are facing one crisis after another while Jesus Christ contends He has the solution to all of them. Christ is concerned about your attitude in dealing with problems.

In light of Jesus' prayer in the most critical hour of His life, let us be willing to lay aside ourselves by trusting Him to give us unity in our homes, churches, businesses, and other relationships. By trusting Him, we will prove that the unity which is good for a basketball team is also good for our personal lives.

The discord and frustration plaguing our society show that unity does not come naturally. It is a prized possession. Building unity in any situation is not easy. Any married couple will be quick to state that it requires work to have a good marriage.

Christianity is to be lived each day. Jesus died on the cross to give us eternal life, but this is only the beginning; He promised abundant life in JOHN 10:10. If we are not receiving this abundant life, Jesus is a liar or we are doing something wrong. We can be sure Jesus' words are true because *"All Scripture is inspired by God"* (**2 TIMOTHY 3:16 NASB**). The individual who is not experiencing life in abudance is not following God's principles for successful living.

In 1963, I purchased a Volkswagen. I was proud of my new car but soon realized I needed to rely on the instruction manual, because I knew very little about Volkswagens. One day I had a flat tire, and without the instruction manual I would never have been able to figure out how to use the jack. Time and again the manual saved me from serious mistakes.

When I made the wonderful discovery of knowing Jesus Christ in a personal way, not only did I begin an exciting adventure with Him, but I received an instruction manual to tell me how to experience the abundant life He talked about. I found God's Word was much like my Volkswagen manual. When I followed the Volkswagen manual meticulously, my car performed well.

"All Scripture...is profitable for teaching, for reproof, for correction, for training in righteousness; that the man of God may be adequate, equipped for every good work" (**2 TIMOTHY 3:16-17 NASB**). The words appeared to leap off the pages at me. I wanted to be equipped to do good works. As I allowed my mind to drift back over my activities, it was obvious I was successful in those areas where I had followed Scriptural principles. Following that old adage, "When you find a good thing, run with it," I became eager to apply more of God's principles to my life.

Apply God's principles to your life, and I am confident you will find *"the unity of the Spirit in the bond of peace"* (**EPHESIANS 4:3**). Because Jesus taught that our goal is to reflect the oneness that only He can produce in our marriages, families, churches, and other organizations, we must be as specific and practical as possible.

SCRIPTURAL PRINCIPLES

1. HONESTY

"Lies will get any man into trouble, but honesty is its own defense" (**PROVERBS 12:13 TLB**). In the name of love, courtesy, or charity, we do not want to tell the whole truth. One of my college professors had a favorite saying, "Look out for those 'but' people." He was referring to the guy who would say, "Joe is really a great guy, but--." Then the verbal attack would come. The initial remarks meant

nothing, and they were used to introduce the negative remarks. Talking behind people's backs is a form of dishonesty.

In **MATTHEW 18:15-20** and **GALATIANS 6:1-6**, God has given us a procedure for handling personal relationships. For instance, suppose a Christian brother has offended you, perhaps deliberately. Specific steps to use in building the unity of the Spirit with him are:

- Go with a humble spirit to the individual who is wronging you and speak with him privately.

- Be willing to accept your part of the blame as well as the other person's. Attitudes are more important than being right.

- If you get no results by yourself, take one or two mature persons with you.

By applying these rules in daily living situations, you will experience a healthier attitude toward life.

I make it a point to let my close friends and associates know that I try to live by these standards. I let them know I will not allow them to talk about others around me unless they are willing to offer solutions, and I ask them to hold me to the same practice, should I fall into critical discussion of another. Will you do the same?

2. UNSELFISHNESS

"Do nothing out of selfish ambition or vain conceit, but in humility consider others better than yourselves. Each of you should look not only to your own interests, but also to the interests of others" (PHILIPPIANS 2:3-4).

There is much truth in the cliché, "The key to joy is Jesus, others, and yourself." Most of our problems stem from selfishness. Selfishness causes us to be people-oriented rather than Christ-oriented. For example, the Bible teaches that men are to love their wives unconditionally. This love is not dependent upon her response. Some will protest that it is impossible to love someone who does not return love, but God in His infinite wisdom has all the answers. He has made women to be responders, and they will respond in love to unconditional love.

Not long ago, I was speaking to a dean of education at a western university. This educated man did not believe in Christ as his Savior, but he realized man's only hope for inner peace and freedom was to become unselfish. This logic is certainly true, but it is one thing to desire to be unselfish and quite another matter to become so. The only place one dies to self is at the cross of Jesus Christ. The apostle Paul experienced this death. He said, *"I have been crucified with Christ: and I myself no longer live, but Christ lives in me. And the real life I now have within this body is a result of my trusting in the Son of God, who loved me and gave Himself for me"* **(GALATIANS 2:20 TLB)**.

We must come to the cross daily and die to our selfish ways. When we die to our selfish natures, we actually begin to live. At last we are free and are able to perform our daily tasks without fear of others rejecting us. Another's sour look, ungrateful attitude, or silence no longer offends us because we are free. Our only desire is to glorify Christ through our bodies. Now we realize we can only be responsible for our own actions and not the actions of others. If someone chooses to hate us, that is his privilege. Our responsibility is to love him.

When we yield our lives to Christ, we will experience the victory Babe Pryor discovered when he joined Athletes in Action. He says, "I joined the team because I had a desire to move out and learn to accept the responsibility of living a Christ-centered life. It taught me to sacrifice personal ambitions for the good of larger goals which could only be achieved by yielding my selfish motives in favor of team unity."

Let's be Christ-oriented people, not people-oriented. Joy comes from Jesus, not from people or things.

3. WILLINGNESS TO REPENT

Have you ever considered on what basis God forgives some of His people and not others? Abraham certainly was not perfect, but he became "the father of many nations." David was guilty of adultery and murder, but God called David a man after His own heart. Why?

On the other hand, God called Saul out of the fields to be the first king of Israel. Initially Saul was a very humble man, but as he grew in stature and prestige, he became a law unto himself. Eventually, Saul was beheaded by the

Philistines after God turned His back on him. Why did Saul lose the blessing of the Lord?

I am confident the following Scriptures will answer these questions. In 1 Samuel 15, we read that Saul disobeyed God and then blamed the sin on the people when questioned about it. In contrast, David openly confessed his sin.

"What happiness for those whose guilt has been forgiven! What joys when sins are covered over! What relief for those who have confessed their sins and God has cleared their record. There was a time when I wouldn't admit what a sinner I was. But my dishonesty made me miserable and filled my days with frustration. All day and all night Your hand was heavy on me. My strength evaporated like water on a sunny day until I finally admitted all my sins to You and stopped trying to hide them. I said to myself, 'I will confess them to the Lord.' And You forgave me! All my guilt is gone. Now I say that each believer should confess his sins to God when he is aware of them, while there is time to be forgiven. Judgment will not touch him if he does" (PSALM 32:1-6 TLB).

The Bible has a lot to say about repentance. Repent means to change. *"If we confess our sins, He is faithful and just and will forgive us our sins and purify us from all unrighteousness"* (1 JOHN 1:9). In Revelation 2 and 3, Jesus very pointedly warns each of the seven churches to have an ear so they will hear and repent, or else they will be destroyed.

God knows that none of us is perfect, but He certainly expects us to genuinely ask forgiveness. If you sin against your fellowman, you need to ask his forgiveness. Notice I did not say apologize or say you are sorry. It is far easier to tell an offended brother you are sorry than it is to ask forgiveness. When you ask someone to forgive you, you have made yourself vulnerable, because this requires a response by the other person. He can choose to refuse to forgive you. Never say, "If I was wrong, will you forgive me?" or "I will forgive you if you will forgive me." The Bible tells us to never allow the sun to go down without settling our differences (EPHESIANS 4:26).

A youth worker once took a poll among teenagers, asking them to list the characteristics they would most like to see changed in their fathers. The two far above the rest were "I wish my father did not lose his temper," and "I wish my father would admit it when he is wrong."

If you are harboring bitterness or resentment toward anyone, seek God's forgiveness right now. Then seek the forgiveness of any person you resent. God loves you so much He does not want bitterness and resentment to destroy you. Seeking forgiveness is not a sign of weakness, but a powerful demonstration of spiritual maturity.

Honesty, unselfishness, and forgiveness are essential to unity. However, I have omitted the most important quality of all. Without it, unity is not possible. The next chapter will be devoted to this subject. When man discovers the answer Jesus provides, he has found the greatest source of power ever known.

PROJECT 3

Study John 17, especially verses 20-22 and 26. Any relationship involving two or more people is a team. It would be helpful to list all the teams in which you have a part. Analyze your contribution to the unity of that team. Consider family, business, church, clubs, athletic teams, etc.

Underline those words that are true of your life: loner, quiet, gossip, dishonest, critical, harsh, stubborn, unforgiving, uncomplimentary, selfish, inferiority complex, forgetful, irresponsible, procrastinator, often late, temper, irritable.

Each of the above is detrimental to harmony and unity. Isolate your weaknesses and each day concentrate on doing the opposite of your weaknesses.

If a friend is one who will tell you what you need to hear and not necessarily what you want to hear, how many friends do you have? Interpersonal relationships would improve one hundred percent if we would be faithful to the principles set forth in MATTHEW 18:15-20.

List the three steps in solving problems. Hopefully, each of us will be honest by not gossiping or allowing others to gossip in our presence.

1)

2)

3)

Read MATTHEW 5:22-24, MATTHEW 6:14-15, AND GALATIANS 6:1. Seeking another's forgiveness is not a sign of weakness, but a powerful display of maturity. We can never guarantee we will not fail in the future, but we can guarantee a repentant and forgiving heart.

If you have bitterness and resentment toward another person, or if you have wronged someone, please remove these barriers immediately by asking God's forgiveness and going humbly to the person involved. Don't use any excuses!

Current Reflections

Oh, to return to the prosperity of the 1960s! Yet, they were not perfect years. Our nation was gripped in a fierce war. Vietnam was a divider of our nation. Racial tensions in America were intense. "Burn, baby, burn" was the cry of dissident Americans. The hippie culture was the introduction to rampant use of illegal drugs.

In spite of the 1960s' turbulent times, they seem insignificant compared to the problems our world faces today. Hatred and violence, death and destruction, fear and disunity abound on every continent, in every nation, in every community; in schools, churches, businesses and, unfortunately, in too many homes.

Team building was my most difficult challenge in the '60s. Still, today, it is my most difficult challenge. It has not changed. It has only become more difficult. Why? I wish I had the answers. Thirty-three years ago I felt I had all the answers, just as today there are success formulas for everything. (We think life is meant to be logical!)

Today, I confess I do not have all the answers. (And maybe I don't even know all the questions!) However, I am able to tell you this. Team unity is costly. Unity in the family is costly. Unity in schools and businesses is costly. Unity in Christianity is costly. Living at peace with all people, so far as it is possible, is costly. To put it mildly, team unity has an enormous price tag.

As Jesus prepared to die a painful death, He prayed for every person who loves Him to be united—united so that the world would believe that God sent Jesus to earth. Is it any wonder the vast majority of the world rejects the message of Jesus Christ?

In 1966, my aspiration was to change the world. Today, my goal is not as grandiose. My prayer is, "Lord, change me so that I can best serve You by loving others. Help me be a positive member of my teams." This chapter convicts me even thirty-three years after writing the book. For me, retirement is out of the question. My prayer is not fully accomplished.

Chapter Notes

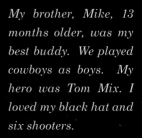

My brother, Mike, 13 months older, was my best buddy. We played cowboys as boys. My hero was Tom Mix. I loved my black hat and six shooters.

School was fun for me because of my love for sports and being with friends. This photo reminds me of the happy days I had living in Anacortes, the gateway to the San Juan Islands in Washington State.

There have been some special basketball teams in my life, both as a player and coach. The 1960 Anacortes High School basketball team was the most important team. In the first grade, many of us began dreaming about winning a state championship. Still today, several of us meet yearly. This was a great team and a group of special people. (Fred is seated 7th from right to left.)

Basketball was by far the most important thing in my life. Playing in big games made life exciting. The jumper against Everett High in 1959-60 was one of those big games.

The score was tied 21 times before we finally won 59-55. To this day, I am asked how I can remember scores and financial numbers. I wonder, too, when I can't remember the three things Susie wants me to bring home from the store.

June 9, 1963, was the greatest day in my life when Susie King said, "I do" at our wedding ceremony in Coeur d' Alene, Idaho. One of the core values I share with young men is, "Always marry someone better than yourself." I am the king of marrying far above myself.

I love this picture of Susie holding one of our grandchildren. If a picture is worth a thousands words in this photo, I see a lifetime of partnering with one of the finest people I know. Susie is a gifted college professor, a master of home decoration and clothing expertise, and more importantly, a mother and grandmother extraordinaire.

Without hesitation the jewels in the Crowell family crown are Jennifer and Jay. Jennifer, whom I call Glory, was always our resident butterfly. Jay, the Oarsman, was our second miracle. (An oarsman in my view is a work horse, a get-it-done guy.) It took 17 years of marriage to get our second heavenly gift. Both Jennifer and Jay live lives of professional excellence, are committed to family unity, and serve our world with compassion.

Our Jennifer became the beloved wife of Dr. Shann Ferch. Jennifer Love blessed us by saying yes to Jay. Life is very good when your children marry well. We are richly blessed.

MEET MY HEAD COACH

Susie says, "We would have skipped parenthood if we would have known how wonderful it is to be grandma and poppa. Natalya, age 10; Ariana, age 4; and Isabella, age 2, are the delights of our lives. The best part is we live a three-minute walk from their home. My hot tub is just around the corner and always ready.

The greatest resource in America is youth; the most neglected is the elderly. Susie and I are thankful we can become as children each year at Disneyland with our amazing grandaughters.

It is quite an honor and privilege to be able to say my best male friend in the world is my son, Jay. My second best friend is my son-in-law, Shann. Both are sensational basketball players. More importantly, they are men any young boy aspiring to greatness could model their life after and be well pleased with the results.

Lyle Patterson is one of the finest men I know. Lyle is what we call "a national treasure." He was a B-29 gunner in the Korean War. Anytime Lyle is available, I ask him to tell his life story. He grew up during the great depression. Lyle never saw his parents after age five. He gunned down a Russian MiG. Coach Patterson won 624 high school basketball games, had the Naselle High School gymnasium named after him and is a member of the Washington State Coaches Hall of Fame. Lyle and Elaine have been married 51 years. They truly love family and God with all their hearts.

The mark of greatness is often related to the people you hang out with or look to for counsel. Jim Harrick, John Wooden and Lyle Patterson are three of the best basketball coaches in the world. I had the privilege of going to John Wooden's home with Jim Harrick. Wooden, in my view, has no equal in the world of basketball coaching. Harrick has won everywhere he has ever coached.

MEET **MY**
HEAD
COACH

7

POWER PLAY

“

This is, without doubt, the best book I have read in my life. For me, it beats Aquinas, Augustine, Lewis, all the greats, for the simple reason that it took my entrenched skepticism and turned it into faith. I had spent ten years wrestling with spiritual questions, always unable to take the ultimate step. But when I put down Fred's book after several hours of non-stop reading, something had clicked, and I invited Christ into my life. It was a moment I shall never, ever forget.

I couldn't tell you how it happened exactly, but I think I had finally understood that believing in something was not intellectual suicide. I understood that I had to let go. Fred made this possible by speaking to both my heart and my mind. Before I picked up this book, I was intellectually, but not spiritually engaged. I was familiar with all the arguments for Christianity, but a crucial element was still missing. This book brought my intellect and my spirit together. It engaged my entire being, which allowed me to experience authentic belief for the first time.

What impacted me the most was the way Fred grounded the case for Christianity in real, everyday life. The interplay between narrative and scripture persuaded me that Christianity could provide the answer to every question thrown up by life. The fact that I could identify areas of my own life that would benefit from the application of biblical principles led me to see Christianity as profoundly relevant. It made me want to be a better person. The day after I had read this book and become a Christian, I asked my mother for her forgiveness for my years of anger and resentment, which was a powerful moment for us both.

The point is that Christianity came alive to me in this book. It became real, attractive, and far more than just a religion. I used to see religion as a control and a constraint. What I discovered in this book was a relationship that was guiding, directing, and empowering people towards goodness. I felt very drawn to that. When I read that Christ was concerned with our attitude while dealing with problems, I realized that this was a higher and more fulfilling standard. It all made such perfect sense.

The genius of *Meet My Head Coach* is that it is, quite literally, an introduction to Jesus Christ Himself. Something about this book opened up my heart. I find it difficult to pinpoint exactly what it was; except to say that it felt like my spirit was being nourished and emboldened with every word I read, as though it had been waiting for the wisdom I was reading. I think the model of Christian love portrayed in the book was a big factor in my conversion— perhaps the biggest. Yes, love is what drew me to Christianity from the very beginning. This book moved me from a vague idea of Christianity to a strong sense of Christ. That is the true genius of Fred's book. Whereas other books had introduced me to Christianity, Fred introduced me to Christ.

RAKIYA ELE FAY

RAKIYA ELE FAY LIVES IN LONDON WITH HER FAMILY. SHE GRADUATED FROM UNIVERSITY COLLEGE LONDON WITH A FRENCH DEGREE AND WENT ON TO EARN A POSTGRADUATE DEGREE FROM THE LONDON SCHOOL OF JOURNALISM. HER STUDIES ALSO INCLUDE ONE YEAR AT THE SORBONNE UNIVERSITY IN PARIS. SHE WAS SELECTED FROM AMONG 2,000 CANDIDATES TO WORK IN THE PRESS SERVICE OF THE EUROPEAN PARLIAMENT IN BRUSSELS. IN 1995, SHE RECEIVED THE MOST VALUABLE PERSON AWARD AT THE UK NBC CAMPS. SINCE THEN, SHE HAS REMAINED INVOLVED WITH THE CAMPS AS A SUMMER COACH.

A re you a Christian?" asked the beautiful, young, South American woman. Jimmie Walker, one of our outstanding basketball players, responded to her question by saying, "Yes. Are you?"

"Yes, but I am not clean," was her reply.

By this time Jimmie was confused, because he could not understand her broken English. I was talking to a young man through our interpreter, Norm Mydske, a missionary living in Lima, Peru. Norm had arranged our entire South American tour. Jimmie came to tell us he could not help this lady because of the language barrier. This sounded important, so Norm went with Jimmie to counsel with the young lady. The teenager I was talking to could write English better than he could speak, so we continued our conversation on paper. Before we finished, he asked Christ to come into his life as Savior.

Meanwhile, Norm and Jimmie were listening to the young lady say she could no longer listen, night after night, to our basketball players as they talk about the love, peace, and joy they were experiencing without finding these same qualities for herself. We had played in three different cities in Chile, each many miles from the others, so Norm was amazed she had seen all three games. He wanted to know how this was possible.

"I am too ashamed to tell you," was her response.

Then reluctantly, in a sea of tears, this attractive lady of about 21 told how she was the mistress of an official who guided our team from city to city. She had been raised in a Christian home, but in order to pursue a career in music, she had fallen into deep sin. Norm gently told her what she must do to find peace with God, but she was very frightened and lonely.

"I know what I must do," she said, "because living the way I am now is horrible. I look like I am alive, but in reality I am dead."

Our team began to pray for her to break off this relationship and seek God's forgiveness. Three days later she spent the day weeping over her sins until she could cry no more. Then she went to church to ask for God's forgiveness and promise Him she would go home to her family.

The apostle Paul could understand the feelings of a sinner because he was guilty of murder. He was able to say, *"When someone becomes a Christian, he becomes a* brand new person inside. He is not the same any more. A new life has begun!" (2 **CORINTHIANS** 5:17 **TLB**). This great man of God went on to say, "For Christ's love controls us now..." (2 **CORINTHIANS** 5:14 **TLB**). Yes, the love of Christ reaches out to us all regardless of our lifestyle, and by yielding to Him, our lives are transformed.

I enjoy talking about love more than anything else because I have seen God's love change my life and others' over the past seven years. This young South American girl is just one who no longer wanted to go on living without experiencing the love and joy only Christ can provide.

In John 17, which we already studied, Jesus concludes this beautiful prayer by giving love as a necessity for unity. "I have made You known to them, and will continue to make You known in order that the love You have for Me may be in them and that I myself may be in them" (**JOHN** 17:26).

It is impossible to study the Bible without reading about the necessity to love others in order to be a mature Christian. There are over 300 references in the Bible dealing with love. "The goal of this command is love, which comes from a pure heart and a good conscience and a sincere faith" (1 **TIMOTHY** 1:5). "Let all that you do be done in love" (1 **CORINTHIANS** 16:14 **NASB**). "...Therefore love is the fulfillment of the law" (**ROMANS** 13:10).

When He was asked what was the greatest of God's commandments, Jesus answered, "'Love the Lord your God with all your heart and with all your soul and with all your mind.' This is the first and greatest commandment. And the second is like it: 'Love your neighbor as yourself.' All the Law and the Prophets hang on these two commandments" (**MATTHEW** 22:37-40).

In light of our changing times, it is interesting to consider that Jesus quoted from the Old Testament. God revealed this important principle of love in the book of Deuteronomy around 1400 B.C. (**DEUTERONOMY** 6:5). It is still true today.

Jesus gives three distinct commands in this Scripture. These are: love God, love your neighbor, and love yourself. The majority of people who are experiencing difficulty in the Christian life are violating one or more of these three fundamental commands. I pray that the Holy Spirit will give you new understanding as we carefully examine these three commands, because the key to a healthy, vital relationship with the Lord Jesus Christ is directly related to our understanding of love.

LOVE GOD

Wherever I travel with the basketball team, I find people who have a distorted picture of God. They invariably picture God as someone who is always going to punish them the minute they get out of line. All too often people think Christianity is some great experience which enables a person to give up everything fun in a desire to live as a stoic, depriving himself of all the enjoyable things in life.

Where do people get this idea of God? I find no place in Scripture where God is just around the corner with a big, ugly stick, waiting to hit me when I sin. I read in the Bible and experience in my life that God is love. Doesn't the Bible say, *"For God so loved the world that He gave His one and only Son"* (JOHN 3:16) The apostle John, who was exiled to die on the Isle of Patmos, wrote, *"We need have no fear of someone who loves us perfectly; his perfect love for us eliminates all dread of what he might do to us. If we are afraid, it is for fear of what he might do to us, and shows that we are not fully convinced that he really loves us"* (1 JOHN 4:18 TLB). This is strong testimony of God's love.

I personally do not believe God gave us commandments and principles to follow to justify punishing us for disobedience. I view these standards as a further expression of His love for me. God loves me so much that He wants me to live happily and successfully. For example, He does not condone premarital sex. When a young girl gets pregnant, the natural consequences of her act are her punishment.

The Bible does explain carefully, however, that God disciplines those He loves. As a parent, I find this same principle true. Because I love my daughter so much, I have no alternative but to punish her when she breaks our rules. My daughter can trust me, even though she may experience the rod, because she knows I love her and am only giving her what she needs to be a better person. In the same way, we can trust our heavenly Father because of his infinite love for us.

One of Satan's most deadly weapons is convincing people they have a faulty relationship with God. Satan, in all his cleverness, endeavors to cause us to doubt God's love by convincing us we can never measure up to God's standards. Consequently, many become defeated and frustrated.

Jesus provides the perfect example to refute Satan's argument. After the resurrection, Jesus showed Himself again to the disciples by the Sea of Tiberias. Initially, the disciples did not recognize Jesus; but there was little doubt after He told them to cast their fishing nets to the right side of the boat, and they could not draw them closed due to the large catch.

After Jesus ate with the men, He asked Peter if he loved Him. Of course, Peter responded with a hearty "yes." Apparently Jesus had a strong point to make because He pressed on, making the same question two more times and causing Peter to become distressed the third time. Each time, Peter said, *"I love you as a dear friend," and Jesus responded, "Feed my sheep"* (JOHN 21:15-17).

This passage reveals Peter could not love Jesus in the same manner that Jesus loved him. Jesus loves unconditionally with no strings attached, but Peter's love was conditional. The love we have for our friends is based on conditional factors, such as personality, actions, and like interests. Yet, in spite of Peter's inability to love Jesus unconditionally, the Lord said, "Feed my sheep." Considering that the number one priority in Jesus' ministry was this, what greater privilege could He give Peter? Jesus knew Peter could not love Him perfectly, and the same is true of us. If we could, we would not need God. Jesus' unconditional love helps me understand that God loves me just as I am. This does not mean He loves sin, but He still loves the sinner.

Psychologists agree the greatest need in the world is love. In his book, Reality Therapy, William Glasser, M.D., states:

> It is generally accepted that all human beings have the same physiological and psychological needs. . .psychology must be concerned with two basic psychological needs: the need to love and be loved, and the need to feel that we are worthwhile to ourselves and to others.

This is not a new discovery, because God created love. When we begin to realize God's unconditional love, we will know He always wants the best for our lives. *"God made Him who had no sin to be sin for us, so that in Him we might become the righteousness of God"* (2 CORINTHIANS 5:21). Praise God and thank Him for making us holy through the Lord Jesus.

LOVE YOUR NEIGHBOR

"I hate my father," were the words of a successful businessman who was experiencing bitterness in his life. This individual proceeded to tell me all the mean things his father had done to him. "Here I am running the entire business, and I never get one compliment or kind word. Every time I make a deal, my father jumps in the middle of it and cusses me out for being stupid. Sometimes I would like to tell him off."

On the surface it would appear this man had every right in the world to hate his father—at least until you read what God has to say about love.

I wanted to help because I could see he was going through much internal strife. To overcome his frustrations, he had a tendency to take them out on his wife and children.

As a result, he was not experiencing the abundant life Christ offers.

When he sought my advice, I asked him when he had last told his father he loved him. Several minutes went by before I received his answer, because a lot of thinking was taking place.

"I can never remember telling my father I loved him," was his reply.

Then I asked him if he loved his father. I was not surprised when he said, "No. Why should I?"

"That is too bad, because you are not being faithful to God," I told him. "Because you do not love your father, you are harboring bitterness and resentment against him. Unfortunately, these unfavorable qualities are making you a very unhappy person. Would you like to resolve your conflict?"

"Yes, I would," was his immediate answer.

"OK. Then pray right now, asking God to give you the ability to love your father."

Sitting in his car, we both bowed in prayer, and this bitter man confessed his sin and asked God to give him love for his father. After our prayer, I asked him if he would be willing to tell his father he loved him the first opportunity that presented itself. He agreed.

I do not know how this story is progressing now between father and son, but I do know I saw the Spirit of God work then as he yielded himself to God. Tears came to his eyes as his heart was freed from bitterness and hate. God loves us so much that He has given us the formula to overcome bitterness and resentment. This formula is love. *"Dear friends, let us practice loving each other, for love comes from God and those who are loving and kind show that they are the children of God, and that they are getting to know Him better. But if a person isn't loving and kind, it shows that he doesn't know God--for God is love"* (1 JOHN 4:7-8 TLB).

Before going any further on this subject of love, I want to give the biblical description of love, because we live in a society which has reduced the concept of love to a lewd scene in the movies. For many it is impossible to separate love and sex, but according to the Bible, sexuality is just one of many expressions of love.

The best definition of love I have ever heard is, "Love is giving people what they need." Paul does an excellent job of describing love in his first letter to the church in Corinth. These are the biblical characteristics of love:

> *Love is patient.*

> *Love is kind.*

> *Love is not jealous or envious.*

> *Love does not brag.*

> *Love is not rude.*

> *Love is not selfish.*

> *Love is not easily provoked.*

> *Love does not think evil.*

> *Love does not rejoice in sin, but rejoices in truth.*

Understanding the definition and characteristics of love is important, but this knowledge is meaningless if we are not willing to put love into practice. Again we must look at the life of Jesus Christ for an example, because He provides the perfect model. Jesus not only demonstrated love through acts of kindness, but verbally communicated His love on a regular basis to those about Him. This provides us with our model! We need to demonstrate our love through our actions, and we need to verbalize it.

I have made it a practice to ask men if their fathers ever said that they loved them. To my amazement, I have found less than five men who have heard their fathers say, "Son, I want you to know that I love you." Is this true of your experience? Why is it so difficult for parents to utter these words? Does it not seem tragic considering God talks about love being our greatest need? Recently I was teaching in a home Bible study, and one of the men said, "If I told my son I loved him, he would think I had taken leave of my senses." How tragic!

I also began experimenting by verbalizing my love to other people. One evening, my wife and I were invited to the home of friends for dinner. They had a cute little boy about two years old sitting next to me at the table. He was quite talkative, and we had a good time chatting. I decided to try my experiment. I said, "Brett, do you want to know something?" His eyes widened, and he said, "Yes."

"I really love you."

Brett's face lit up, and he was so excited he nearly wriggled his way out of the chair. Four simple words, but what an impact they made.

Several months later I was traveling with the basketball team in Texas, and I stayed in the home of a dentist. One evening Bill and I were having some wonderful fellowship after his family had gone to bed. We had prayed together, and when I stood up I shook Bill's hand and said, "Bill, God loves you, and I love you." Tears came to his eyes as he told me this was the first time in his life that another man had ever said he loved him. It was obvious this was a very meaningful experience to Bill because I was communicating God's love to him.

I want to be careful not to lead you to believe I advocate running around telling everyone you love him or her. In every area of spiritual truth, we must exercise balance and depend upon the leading of the Holy Spirit. It may be very difficult for some to verbalize their feelings toward others. The tragedy occurs when we are not willing to verbalize our love to our spouse and children. Many a wife goes through married life never hearing a husband say "I love you" after the courtship years.

If you are one of those who say this is not important, you have missed the ball game. Jesus said, "Love thy neighbor," and if you love your neighbor more than your wife, you are in serious trouble. All of us know words can come cheaply, so we must back up our words by our actions. One of the most meaningful projects I have ever undertaken, and it bears repeating, has been living **HEBREWS 10:24 NASB**: *"And let us consider how to stimulate one another to love and good deeds."*

After five years of marriage, our first child was born. It was obvious there were two babies in our house—myself and our little girl, Jennifer. Initially, I thought I was above changing diapers and washing clothes, but God began to convict me.

I began asking myself, Why won't you do these mundane chores when Susie is busy and you are lying on your back? You see, it was easy for me to lie on the couch and say, "Susie, I really love you," but God also wanted me to demonstrate this love in specific acts of love. By applying this verse of Scripture, I began to realize my testimony was not worth much when I was not willing to do little things for my wife—trivial acts like opening the car door, taking out the garbage, and being sensitive to her needs.

As you examine your own life, how do you rate yourself in verbalizing and demonstrating your love to others, especially your family? Dad, when was the last time you put your arm around your wife and told her you love her? How about your children? The next time you look at them, remember their greatest need in life is to experience love—your love!

LOVE YOURSELF

I am sure you are prepared to hear a few kind words about the importance of self-acceptance and then the usual routine about esteeming others higher than yourself. I'm sorry, but I plan to do everything possible to get under your skin, because I believe the concept of self-love is one of the most violated principles of Scripture. In fact, I would be hard pressed to say which is more important—loving self or loving God. That statement ought to put me in the theological woodshed! Before you turn me off, give me an opportunity to present my case.

On the basis of my experience in counseling and evangelistic work, I find a direct relation between a person's self-image and his ability to accept Christ. The individual who hates himself has difficulty understanding and accepting God's love. His reasoning goes something like this, "If God made this mess, I sure don't want to have anything to do with Him." These self-haters also have difficulty accepting the love of relatives and friends. I have told people in counseling situations that "God loves you, and I love you," but they look at me as though I couldn't be telling the truth. They want to believe me, but their experiences tell them it isn't true.

You may have difficulty accepting this. Do not take my word for it. The following statistics speak for themselves. (As shocked as I was about these 1971 statistics, they pale in comparison to the shocking moral decline we face years later with these statistics multiplied).

There are approximately 22,000 suicides per year in the U.S., or one suicide every twenty-four minutes.

There are 1,361,000 people in mental hospitals, institutions, psychiatric clinics and as out patients in the U.S.

There are more than 8,000,000 alcoholics in the U.S. and 350,000 alcoholics die each year. (They need to know that someone cares about them, not just their problem.)

Surveys of college coeds show that ninety percent are dissatisfied in some way with their appearance. (Self-rejection or dissatisfaction quickly transfers into an attitude of "others don't like me," increasing fear and isolation.)

Approximately 1,500 teenagers run away from home every day, or 547,500 each year. (Generally they no longer felt loved, wanted or accepted. They were estranged from their own parents.)

Dr. Grant Gwinup, University of California, at Irvine states, "Eighty-five percent of the adult population in the U.S. is overweight and carrying five billion pounds of excess fat." (Many eat because they feel lonely and unaccepted.)

Statistics do not always tell the truth, but I believe those above paint a clear picture of the complicated problems people are facing. I have never met anyone with confidence, poise, a good self-image, and humble love for self, who resorted to an escape in alcohol, drugs, sex, or suicide. As these statistics reveal, not loving oneself can have a devastating effect on one's life. You may be saying, "I am not an alcoholic, dope addict, and have never attempted suicide; therefore, I must love myself." This is not necessarily true.

Those who cannot accept themselves, generally seek experience after experience, attempting to satisfy themselves. I can immediately think of three common ways to do this. Some people always look ahead to the next big event—vacation, ball game—and do not enjoy living for each day. Others constantly buy things that never satisfy; they try to bury their inferiority complex in their possessions, or hide it behind a new outfit for every party. And others always say that everything will be OK when they leave here or this job. They always find more problems waiting wherever they go. God wants us to learn how to solve problems, not run from them. Maybe you see yourself in one or more of these areas.

The primary reason we cannot love ourselves is due to selfishness. All too often we assume self-love and self-centeredness are synonymous. We need to divorce ourselves from the thought that self-love is demonstrated by the boisterous egotist telling everyone how wonderful he is. Conceit is a symptom of an inferiority complex.

According to Webster, selfishness can be defined as devoted to or caring for self; influenced solely or chiefly by consideration of personal interest. In *The Art of Loving*, Erich Fromm states:

"The affirmation of one's own life, happiness, growth, freedom is rooted in one's capacity to love. If an individual is able to love productively, he loves himself, too; if he can love only others he cannot love at all. The selfish person is interested only in himself, wants everything for himself, feels no pleasure in giving, but only in taking. . .Does not this prove that concern for others and concern for oneself are unavoidable alternatives? This would be so if selfishness and self-love were identical. But that assumption is the very fallacy which has led to so many mistaken conclusions concerning our problem. Selfishness and self-love, far from being identical, are actually opposites. The selfish person does not love himself too much but too little; in fact, he hates himself. This lack of fondness and care for himself, which is only one expression of his lack of productiveness, leaves him empty and frustrated. It is true that selfish persons are incapable of loving others, but they are not capable of loving themselves either."

In order to experience joy in living, selfishness must be removed from our lives. As Dr. Fromm said, selfish people cannot love others, and they cannot love themselves.

Let me ask you a personal question. Do you love yourself? If you could look in a mirror and change anything, what would you like to change? Since even Hollywood's most glamorous movie stars would like to change their appearances, I am sure you would like to make some changes. I do not have a magic solution for you, but I would like to share some of God's principles which are better than any physical change you could ever experience.

The first step in self-acceptance is to see yourself as God sees you. In the Psalms, we find David saying, *"I praise You because I am fearfully and wonderfully made; Your works are wonderful, I know that full well"* (PSALM 139:14). God is still at work perfecting you in order that you might reflect the love of Christ through your life. What a wonderful privilege. Once we understand God's view, we realize our lives are like a picture in a frame. A frame has only one purpose, and that is to complement the picture. The frame should never draw attention away from the picture. In like manner, our bodies are frames and our total personality is the picture. When we realize this, we're on the way to becoming one of the "beautiful people." According to the apostle Paul, God says, *"It is God Himself who has made us what we are and given us new lives from Christ Jesus; and long ages ago He planned that we should spend these lives in helping others"* (EPHESIANS 2:10 TLB).

I appreciate the privilege of writing about two of those "beautiful people" who have influenced my life. One lady is my wife's grandmother, but I have adopted her as my own grandmother. She is in her eighties and espouses the philosophy, "I want to wear out, not rust out." For her eighty-fourth birthday, her children gave her a push lawnmower! It is great to be around her because she is happy, smiling, and deeply interested in others. Never have I heard her utter an unkind word about anyone. She is not worried about her appearance, the big event next week, or the problems she might face, because she allows Christ to live through her life. Grandma Williams is just one of those beautiful people.

The second of those beautiful people I would like to tell you about is my Uncle Walt. His life is the personification of Christ's teaching that if you serve, you will be served, love and you will be loved, and give and you will receive. Uncle Walt serves, loves, and gives without expecting anything in return. His appreciative attitude, genuine interest in people, and giving spirit draw people to him. Consequently, others enjoy doing nice things for him. Uncle Walt is one of those people that make the Apostle Paul's admonition to his Philippian friends easy to follow. *"Whatever you have learned or received or heard from me, or seen in me--put it into practice and the God of peace will be with you"* (PHILIPPIANS 4:9, 10).

PROJECT 4

Take time to evaluate your personal love for God, for self, and for others. Which area needs work? Be specific.

Learning to love God will be evident in your life as you begin to view your heavenly Father as one who truly loves you. Read the following chapters in the Bible: JOHN 1-3, ROMANS 5, 1 JOHN 4. Then begin to thank God for His love for you and verbalize your love for Him.

Much of loving others requires a warm heart, but it also requires learning specific skills. COLOSSIANS 3:17 says, *"And whatever you do, whether in word or deed, do it all in the name of the Lord Jesus, giving thanks to God the Father through Him."* Begin by memorizing HEBREWS 10:24. Then spend three to five minutes daily listing ways to love other members of your family or friends. For example, my brother:

- *Listen when he speaks.*
- *Compliment him when he does something well.*
- *Help him cut the grass or wash the car.*

Read 1 CORINTHIANS 13 every day for a month. Select one virtue of love each day and put it into practice. For example, love is patient. Ask God to enable you to be patient. Build each of these attributes into your life.

Begin to love self by faith. First, make two columns—one column including those qualities you can change; the other column including those areas of your life you cannot change. For example:

CHANGEABLES	UNCHANGEABLES
50 lbs. overweight	Too tall
Temper	Big nose
Laziness	Too short
Resentment	Illness

For those you cannot change, apply 1 THESSALONIANS 5:18, but get busy with a specific program to eliminate the changeables. Get a piece of paper. Define the specific problem; then list specific steps to eliminate the problem.

Secondly, read PROVERBS 15:23 and PHILIPPIANS 4:8. These verses challenge us to concentrate on the positive. People who do not love themselves are continually degrading themselves. If this is true of your life, eliminate destructive self-criticism. Every time you realize you are being critical, ask God's forgiveness and fill the void with positive thoughts about self. If you are being irresponsible, do not wallow in self-pity, but correct the behavior.

Current Reflections

"But God demonstrates His own love for us in this: While we were still sinners, Christ died for us" (ROMANS 5:8). When I embraced that love forty years ago, I did not know that love would be continually and daily outpoured to me. All these years, the learning curve has been long and steep. It is my conviction that God will spare no measure to prove to us how much He loves us.

What I further did not comprehend at that point in my faith journey was that faith and suffering go hand-in-hand. Meet a person with great compassion and humility, and you will most likely discover a person who has suffered either a loss or pain. No one empathizes with cancer victims like a cancer victim himself; no one is more committed to drug abuse counseling than the recovering addict; no one prizes a wonderful family more than the one who has experienced healing from a damaged family.

Fortunately for me, God did not reveal the dark waters I would pass through to become the person I am today. Above all else, my "undergirding" anchor has been the unconditional love I have experienced through His grace. For forty-five years, my bride and life partner, Susie, has loved and encouraged me. The love from my family, numerous friends, business associates and staff motivates me to face the future with gratitude and extend that kind of love to others.

The winter days of Susie's and my life will be the true testing grounds of this love of which I write. My hope is to finish strong loving my God, loving people, loving life, and even loving me, which is often the most difficult.

Chapter Notes

MEET MY
HEAD COACH

8

SMILE, COACH, GOD LOVES YA!

"

For the last few years, I have been powerfully blessed with the presence of Fred Crowell in my life, both as his spiritual director and friend. We have had many hours of spiritual conversations, as well as personal dialogues, in the context of deepening friendship. I have seen Fred as a man of great faith; as a father who is richly blessed with a wonderful wife, daughter, and son; as a grandfather who utterly delights in his grandchildren; as a Spirit-filled, dynamic administrator; as a wise and practical coach; and, very significantly, as a person who animates thousands of young people to deepen themselves in their quest for wholeness and holiness in Christ on a practical level.

Like the apostle Paul, Fred radiates to others the living presence of the Christ-Mind and the Christ-Heart. He truly is a Christ-centered "man for all seasons." In spiritual direction, I have seen him fruitfully pass through a spiritual dark night of the soul and emerge an even stronger man of faith than he was before.

I love Holy Scripture and the memorization of many passages of Scripture, which enrich the treasury of memory and are always available in times of need, as well as times of rejoicing, giving thanks and glorifying God. I have seen Fred delight in psalms and other passages of Scripture which he has added to his own existential treasury of memory. He has also enthusiastically shared this practice with others.

Fred is truly a man of the Bible. He is, in fact, one of the most deeply committed Christians I have ever met. I say this as a Roman Catholic priest who is constantly inspired by Fred to deepen my own spiritual life. In one of the documents of the Society of Jesus to which I belong, it begins with the words: "The Jesuit is a sinner." This certainly fits me all too well, and Fred has magnanimously accepted me with all my flaws. As a wounded healer and spiritual director, I have learned that spiritual direction is never a one-way street. In my encounters with Fred, I can honestly say that I receive as much as, or very often much more than, I give.

One particular quality in Fred that creates a special "holy envy" in me is the endearing way in which he reaches out to everyone he encounters. Within a few minutes, he almost inevitably turns a stranger into someone you would think he has known for years. He always builds up the other person. He spots a good quality in someone, which most of us would miss, and he praises this quality in the person and leaves them in a joyous positive frame of mind. I have seen this happen again and again and again! I praise God for this gift and the many other spiritual virtues Fred has. These virtues all emanate a spirit of peace, assurance, gratitude, and love.

May God hold Fred always in His arms and bless him with an ever more fruitful ministry.

FATHER BERNIE TYRRELL

DR. BERNARD TYRELL, S.J., GREW UP IN YAKIMA, WASHINGTON; HE HOLDS TWO MASTER'S DEGREES, ONE IN PHILOSOPHY AND THE OTHER IN THEOLOGY, AND EARNED HIS DOCTORATE IN PHILOSOPHY FROM FORDHAM UNIVERSITY. AS PROFESSOR EMERITUS IN PHILOSOPHY AND RELIGIOUS STUDIES AT GONZAGA UNIVERSITY, HE HAS HAD A LONG AND SUCCESSFUL TEACHING CAREER. MANY OF HIS STUDENTS, INCLUDING SUSIE CROWELL, CONSIDER FATHER TYRRELL TO BE THE BEST TEACHER OF THEIR EDUCATIONAL YEARS. HIS BOOKS ON CHRISTOTHERAPY HAVE BEEN TRANSLATED INTO LANGUAGES THROUGHOUT THE WORLD.

Athletes in Action played the highly regarded Bowling Green University Falcons during my first year with the team. It was an exciting game all the way, and with only fifteen seconds remaining in the game, we were trailing by only one point. Bowling Green was stalling the basketball, trying to protect the 73-72 lead. Suddenly our star forward Bill Westphal, a graduate of the University of Southern California, made a beautiful steal and quickly dribbled the ball to our goal for an easy two points.

Our bench was in a state of bedlam. We had won the game! Our joy abruptly ended when I saw one of the referees waving his arms to indicate the basket did not count. He had called a foul on Westphal. Instead of our making two points, Bowling Green was awarded two free throws.

As a result of the foul on Westphal, we lost the game 75-72. I was angry. No, I was furious! I wanted to choke that referee. It took every ounce of self-composure I could muster to stand with our players and present our program. It was difficult to congratulate the opposing coach with a smile and not chew out the referees.

Outwardly, I appeared calm, poised, and relaxed, but inwardly I was boiling. By the time I made it to our locker room, I was ready to explode; but much to my surprise, one of our 6'7" centers was standing near the doorway with a huge smile on his face. "Smile, coach, God loves ya!" Mack Crenshaw said.

That was a poor choice of words for Mack. I ignored him. Losing was a bitter pill for me to swallow under any circumstances, but it was pure agony to lose when I knew we should have won. Anyone who isn't sad and silent after losing a game just must not care. However, I knew Mack wanted to win as much as anyone on the team. I could not blame him for lack of interest.

Down deep I admired Mack because he never lost his cool. Even under the most difficult circumstances, he was always in control. Why couldn't I be this way? Since becoming a Christian, I had seen changes. When I began my coaching career four years earlier, I would be sullen for days after losing a game. Yet, I still was not satisfied because I knew losing my temper did not help in any way. It was silly to let trivial things bother me. I would become upset about people being late for meetings, fume when numerous other everyday living situations did not go my way.

As the team traveled to Wisconsin, Illinois, Ohio, Alabama, Oklahoma, and Oregon, I spent a great deal of time thinking about this incident with Mack. I continued to watch Mack carefully because he demonstrated a quality I admired. I wanted to experience the joy, peace, and patience I saw in him.

My hunger to experience this change drove me to study the Bible to find the answers. I soon discovered why I had problems. God clearly establishes that man is basically evil. In Romans we are told, "*There is no one righteous, not even one. . . for all have sinned, and fall short of the glory of God,*" and also, "*For the wages of sin is death; but the gift of God is eternal life through Jesus Christ our Lord*" (ROMANS 3:10, 23, AND 6:23). A life that is man-controlled will exhibit this basic nature.

While studying the fifth chapter of Galatians, I discovered the key to Mack's success. He was allowing God, not self, to control the wellsprings of his being. Paul does an excellent job of contrasting two lives. He begins by listing the activities of the lower nature and concludes by listing the fruits, or results, of being controlled by the Spirit of God. By analyzing these lists, I was able to see the practical application of allowing God to control my entire life. It was obvious that when I was in control of my life, one or more of these unpleasant characteristics manifested itself. On the other hand, one or more of the fruits of the Spirit shone brightly in my life when God was in control.

I challenge you to analyze the contrast Paul makes in GALATIANS 5:16-23.

FRUITS OF THE LOWER NATURE	FRUITS OF THE SPIRIT
SEXUAL IMMORALITY	LOVE
IMPURITY OF MIND	JOY
WORSHIP OF FALSE GODS	PEACE
WITCHCRAFT	PATIENCE
HATRED	KINDNESS
JEALOUSY	FIDELITY
BAD TEMPER	TOLERANCE
RIVALRY, FACTIONS	SELF-CONTROL
DRUNKENNESS, ORGIES	GENEROSITY
QUARRELING	

The apostle Paul tells us that, "*Those who belong to Christ have nailed their natural evil desires to His cross and crucified them there. If we are living now by the Holy Spirit's power, let us follow the Holy Spirit's leading in every part of our lives. Then we won't need to look for honors and popularity, which lead to jealousy and hard feelings*" (GALATIANS 5:24-26 TLB).

More than ever before, I wanted God to control my life. In a small booklet titled, Who Runs Your Life?, I read, "If you squeeze a lemon, you get sour juice. The squeezing did not make the juice sour. It merely brought out what was in the lemon." This same principle applies to us as we face the daily pressures of living. The problems and obstacles we encounter do not make us unhappy, nasty people. They simply bring out our basic nature. This helped me understand that any time Fred Crowell is in control, I can expect a fruit of the flesh to come forth. In Jeremiah we are told "*The heart is deceitful above all things and beyond cure. Who can understand it?*" (JEREMIAH 17:9). The prophet Isaiah said, "*We are the ones who strayed away like sheep! We who left God's paths to follow our own. Yet God laid on Him the guilt and sins of every one of us*" (ISAIAH 53:6 TLB).

For the first time, I began to see with new eyes. Those referees did not make me so angry. People do not make us angry; they only bring out our true nature. Any time we lose control, we should not be surprised when we demonstrate anger, bitterness, jealousy, immorality, and other fruits of the flesh, because these are the natural products of the lower nature.

On a trip to the western United States, I was discussing the Christian life with a college professor. He said, "The key to total fulfillment in life is to become egoless." In other words, he meant to become completely unselfish. I asked him how this was possible. "Self-denial and dedication" was his reply. I do not believe this is a satisfactory answer, because my experience proved self-denial and dedication did not make me totally unselfish. The more I tried to be selfless and calm, the more agitated I became.

The word of God also says self-denial and dedication is not the correct answer. Paul said, "*For what I do is not the good I want to do; no, the evil I do not want to do--this I keep on doing*" (ROMANS 7:19). Paul found the harder he tried to do good the more he did evil.

I am grateful God gives us this answer to man's dilemma. God, in His great wisdom, provides the answer for man's selfishness. His answer is so simple most people miss it.

God teaches we must die to "self" and be controlled by the Spirit. *"For we know that our old self was crucified with Him so that the body of sin might be done away with, that we should no longer be slaves to sin--because anyone who has died has been freed from sin"* (ROMANS 6:6-7). Jesus talked about the necessity of dying. *"The house has come for the Son of Man to be glorified. I tell you the truth, unless a kernel of wheat falls to the ground and dies, it remains only a single seed. But if it dies, it produces many seeds"* (JOHN 12:23-24).

The apostle Paul experienced the reality of becoming controlled by the Spirit. Paul said, *"I have been crucified with Christ: and I myself no longer live, but Christ lives in me. And the real life I now have within this body is a result of my trusting in the Son of God, who loved me and gave himself for me"* (GALATIANS 2:20 TLB).

Never forget that Paul still lived, but he lived by the power and faith of the Son of God. Often, Christians are deceived into believing they are to do nothing; God will do all the work. I remember hearing one of our basketball players asking the Lord to get him in good physical condition for the season. Basketball practice is hard work, involving sweat and pain. Finally, I told the player he could sit on the sidelines all year praying for the Lord to get him in condition, but it just was not going to happen. The Lord will not perform a single miracle unnecessarily. There is one way for a basketball player to get in shape: run, and when he is exhausted, run some more. God blesses those who are willing to step out in faith and claim His promises. I'll address this topic more in the following chapters. I strongly believe in working like everything depended on me and praying like everything depended on God.

"And without faith it is impossible to please God, because anyone who comes to Him must believe that He exists and that He rewards those who earnestly seek Him" (HEBREWS 11:6). By faith we must come to the cross daily and die with Him. I am not talking about becoming a Christian daily, because that only happens once in a lifetime. I am speaking of dying to our lower nature; the lust, envy, bitterness, jealousy, and sin in our lives.

As I began to follow this walk of faith, I experienced new peace and patience. Little nuisances no longer bothered me. When I found myself in tense situations, I began relying upon the resources of God. No, I am not totally dead to self, but I pray as I continue to die to self that I may experience 2 Corinthians 3:18 in totality: *"But we Christians have no veil over our faces; we can be mirrors that brightly reflect the glory of the Lord. And as the Spirit of the Lord works within us, we become more and more like Him"* (2 CORINTHIANS 3:18 TLB).

I am sure you can identify with my past in not experiencing God's joy, peace, and patience. I now find great reward in each day experiencing the happiness and joy resulting from being controlled by God's Holy Spirit. *"Don't cause the Holy Spirit sorrow by the way you live. Remember, he is the one who marks you to be present on that day when salvation from sin will be complete. Stop being mean, bad-tempered and angry. Quarreling, harsh words, and dislike of others should have no place in your lives. Instead, be kind to each other, tenderhearted, forgiving one another, just as God has forgiven you because you belong to Christ"* (EPHESIANS 4:30-32 TLB).

Every Christian desires to be controlled and empowered by the Holy Spirit. I believe the primary reason many do not enjoy this wonderful walk with Christ is due to lack of understanding. If you desire to die to self and to be filled with the Holy Spirit, turn to the second appendix in the back of this book. You will find there a brief article entitled Have You Made the Wonderful Discovery of the Spirit-Filled Life? Dr. Bill Bright wrote this excellent booklet. I have personally seen hundreds of people apply these Scriptural principles to their lives and immediately begin to experience being controlled by the Spirit of God.

The key to living the Christian life is to experience the power of the Holy Spirit. Being controlled by God and being filled with the Spirit is possibly the greatest blessing known to man. In Paul's letter to his dear friend Timothy, we are told, *"For God did not give us a spirit of timidity, but a spirit of power, of love and of self-discipline"* (2 TIMOTHY 1:7). This power that Paul speaks of produces freedom, freedom desperately sought throughout the world, especially by young people.

Since freedom is not the right to do what you want, but the power to do what you should, one can never experience true freedom without the power of the Holy Spirit. Jesus talked about experiencing this power when He said, *"You will know the truth, and the truth will set you free"* (JOHN 8:32). It is folly to believe you are freed by removing all restraints. People do not become free by rejecting responsibility.

To illustrate the fact that man becomes free when he experiences the power to do what he should, I want to share two personal incidents which illustrate freedom and slavery.

The first incident occurred at Western Michigan University. I decided to go to the arena several hours before the basketball game to think about strategy and make sure everything was in order for the half-time program. The local Campus Crusade director, Tom Lumsden, transported me to the game in a late model car and parked quite close to an old panel truck. The truck was in a sorry state: dents, chipped paint, rust. I was very careful as I got out of the car, but in spite of my care, I very gently bumped the truck. There was no damage to either vehicle, but as I walked in front of the panel truck, the young man behind the wheel began screaming obscenities at me. He was furious because I had "damaged" the paint on his truck. I could not believe anyone could be so mad about anything so small. I listened to him and smiled. He then stepped on the accelerator, doing his best to squeal the tires and not quite making it, traveled about twenty feet, came to a screeching halt, popped his head out the window, and let fly another barrage of filthy language. All I could do was smile. Imagine the tension this young man must have been experiencing to react so violently. I wondered how he reacted to serious problems. This man was striving to be free, but unfortunately he was a slave. I felt compassion for him, because he did not have the power to act in a responsible manner.

Several months after this incident in Michigan, we were playing the University of North Dakota. In the second half, one of our best men, Clint Hooper, was injured going for a loose ball. One of our own players accidentally banged him severely on the top of his head and left shoulder. He was not able to remain in the game. However, it did not appear to be a serious injury. We were confident he would be well for our next game with the highly touted University of Missouri. The day of the game arrived, but Clint was unable to use his arm fully. I did not want to use him in the game, even though we desperately needed him, if there was a chance of further injury.

I decided to take Clint to the university's athletic trainer. The trainer examined his back, neck, shoulders, and arms. I watched intently, hoping to pick up his thoughts. Everything was going smoothly until he stood directly behind Clint and asked Clint to lift his arms directly out from his sides to a position above his head. The right arm went through the motion smoothly, but the left arm floundered like a wounded duck.

The trainer's face paled; I sensed trouble. Carefully the trainer said that it appeared to be a very serious condition. One of his players had recently had a similar complaint. If Clint had the same injury, it would take more than a year to completely recover.

What a blow! I nearly became ill. My stomach became tight and quite upset, but Clint only said, "Thank You, Lord. I don't really understand, but thank You anyway." Clint had every reason to lose his self-control. He could have reacted with obscenities or just plain anger, but he was a free man and had the power to respond in a mature manner. Not a word of criticism was uttered.

The trainer made an appointment for us to see one of the finest osteopaths in the country. We went immediately to his office. Our prayer that day was, "Lord, make it possible that an operation will not be necessary." Our joy knew no bounds when the doctor reported that although the problem was severely jolted nerves, proper rest was all that was necessary.

Clint's shoulder did not heal completely until after the basketball season, but he was back in action four days later against Duke University. He scored twenty-two points and demonstrated the reality of Jesus Christ through his sportsmanship.

I have often thought how wonderful it would have been if that young man at Western Michigan University could have experienced the power of the Holy Spirit—a power that would set him free, no longer a slave to daily circumstances.

PROJECT 5

Please turn to the second appendix and read Have You Made the Wonderful Discovery of the Spirit-Filled Life?

Write a brief definition of spiritual breathing as you now understand it. Look at Have You Made the Wonderful Discovery of the Spirit-Filled Life? again to determine the correctness of your answer.

Are you filled with the Holy Spirit?

Yes____ No____ Not sure____

It is exciting to know we do not have to beg God or seek an emotional experience. We can be filled and controlled by the Holy Spirit by faith. Remember **HEBREWS 11:6 TLB** says, *"You can never please God without faith,* *without depending on Him. Anyone who wants to come to God must believe that there is a God and that He rewards those who sincerely look for Him."*

All of us will sin sometime in the future, but we need not remain in sin. Make it a daily practice to confess every known sin and appropriate the filling of His Spirit. If you do not fully understand this wonderful truth, please read Chapter 8 and the material on the Holy Spirit again. Thank God right now for this blessing.

Current Reflections

This chapter brings back so many memories of the victories and failures I have experienced these past thirty-three years. It seems to me two tangibles govern our lives: time and money. Early in my life, I had lots of time and little money. Now I have little time and enough money to live with comfort. Time has definitely become my challenge.

When one has excess time but no money, life becomes very difficult. When one has excess money and no time, death is the reality. Time and money are one and the same in a capitalist society. In Manila, people work for two dollars a day. In the U.S.A., some people make ten dollars an hour, but others make $500 an hour. The point is that time and money drive our lives.

When I originally wrote this book, out of necessity, money was the driver in my life. One year, I had three jobs: academic student counseling at the community college during the day, marriage and family counseling in the evenings, and promoting basketball camps whenever possible. The goal was to pay the mortgage and provide for my family.

My life was in high gear. I was chasing the dream. I disagreed with Thoreau's famous quote, "Most men live lives of quiet desperation." Building the biggest and best basketball camp in the world became my goal. I believed this was God's gift to me and my gift to humanity; I truly thought basketball was my best tool to make a lasting, positive impact upon the youth of this world.

As responsibilities grew and the pace of society quickened, I found myself in a remarkably competitive business world. The one sanctuary I could always rely on to provide the necessary inner resources to compete was my private time with God. There He assured me He was the shepherd of my soul and empowered me with His Spirit. There He became the bigger quest, replaced the restlessness, and brought perspective to my daily life.

Chapter Notes

Chapter Notes

MEET **MY**
HEAD
COACH

9

WHY PRAY TO THE CEILING?

"

Fred Crowell is my hero, confidant, mentor, counselor, business consultant and spiritual teacher. He is also my father. I am proud to be a Crowell because of who my father is and what he stands for.

My father has had a great impact on my life. There is no other man that I love, enjoy, admire and respect more than him. Out of all the many things that Fred Crowell has done for me, the single most important one is that as my earthly father, he has made it easy for me to understand that I have a Heavenly Father who loves me unconditionally, wants the best for me, wants to bless me, and hates to see me go through life's struggles.

I've always been a high achiever academically, athletically, and in business, and therefore find it difficult to not get caught up in my spiritual performance. I think that God loves me and wants to bless my family and me when I am disciplined with my devotions, Bible reading and church attendance. Conversely, when I struggle in my daily devotions or get angry and say something hurtful to my wife, my natural tendency is to feel like I don't deserve God's love and grace. Yet, because of my father's example, I know I can go to my Heavenly Father and ask for forgiveness, and He will welcome me with open arms, as my earthly father has done many times before. My father always loves me and wants the best for me. He always forgives me and accepts me for who I am. He has written thousands of notes of encouragement to me, and has shed tears of sadness or joy, depending on my circumstances. He calls me often to pray with him or give me tips for my business and life. What's more, he is truly committed to being vulnerable with me, which has allowed me to feel comfortable letting him know when he has hurt me, or when I feel he should have handled something differently. My father has made it easy for me to understand what being a father means, and what a father-son relationship looks like. This has been a model to me in my process of submitting my life to my Heavenly Father and in seeking Him as the Lord of my life.

My father has given me a wonderful example for understanding the love of the Father. However, my faith was recently challenged when I read LUKE 11:11-13: *"Which of you fathers, if your son asks for a fish, will give him a snake instead? Or if he asks for an egg, will give him a scorpion? If you then, though you are evil, know how to give good gifts to your children, how much more will your Father in heaven give the Holy Spirit to those who ask Him?"* My father has been so good to me and I've always felt I did not deserve a father like him, yet the Bible is saying he is evil. As I thought over the passage, I realized that if my father on earth, who has loved me and wanted to be nothing more than a great blessing to me, is evil compared to God, what a great, great love the Father must have for me. My dad has shown me by example the goodness of our Heavenly Father and the unconditional love He has for me. I know my dad always wanted to take care of me no matter what my actions deserved. Because of the wonderful example he has set, I am able to accept that God's awesome love is not a reward for good deeds, but simply the love and grace a father has for his child.

JAY CROWELL

JAY CROWELL LIVES IN SEATTLE, WASHINGTON, WITH JENNIFER, HIS WIFE AND BEST FRIEND. HE HAS BEEN A PART OF NBC CAMPS HIS ENTIRE LIFE, FIRST AS A CAMPER, THEN AS A JUNIOR COUNSELOR AND COACH, AND NOW AS A SITE DIRECTOR FOR A FEW WEEKS EACH SUMMER. HE IS A MORTGAGE CONSULTANT IN DOWNTOWN SEATTLE. JAY PLAYED BASKETBALL AT THE UNIVERSITY OF GEORGIA AND GRADUATED WITH HONORS FROM SEATTLE PACIFIC UNIVERSITY WITH A DEGREE IN BUSINESS.

H
oney?"

"Yes?"

"Do you want to pray?"

"No!"

"Why?"

"Because my prayers go no higher than the ceiling!"

This was a typical conversation in our household at bedtime for several weeks. Susie was a new Christian. I was deeply involved in preparing for my second basketball season at the University of Alaska and only mildly interested in Christianity.

Susie did not appreciate my attitude regarding prayer but was careful not to push the issue. She worked in a far more subtle manner—like getting friends to pray for me.

Even after committing my life to Jesus Christ, I must admit group prayer was very difficult. Slowly but surely in spite of my hang-ups, I began to discover the power of prayer. My friend Fred Dyson was an immense help during this early period of growth. Fred was intensely practical with God and could provide realistic answers to my seemingly monumental problems. I am deeply grateful to this man of God because he gave me a model I could imitate. He was the first to demonstrate to me an attractive picture of Christianity.

Dyson's advice revolutionized my thoughts regarding prayer. My concept of prayer was very ritualistic. Since I did not find memorized prayers meaningful, I never prayed. Before talking with Fred, it never occurred to me that prayer was simply talking with God—much like talking with another person.

When I told Fred I did not like to read the Bible or pray, he said, "Tell God."

"What do you mean, 'Tell God'?" I asked.

"Tell God you don't like to talk to Him or read His book. The responsibility to change your attitude is on God, not you. If He wants you to talk with Him, ask Him to give you the desire to pray and to read the Bible."

This concept of prayer was certainly a switch. My first response was one of questioning. Could I actually tell God I was not enthusiastic about talking to Him? Trying to understand this approach logically, I compared talking with God to talking with people.

One of the most lethal weapons in getting revenge is silence. I know people who will not speak for days attempting to get even with another person. Silence also destroys one's relationship with God. Many people give God the silent treatment when they get angry with Him. I know! I was the chief offender. After the death of my mother, I practiced silence with God for over three years.

I began following Fred's advice on prayer. "God, I don't enjoy prayer and Bible reading, but change my attitude and give me a desire to serve You." This approach opened the lines of communication with God. As a result, my life began changing in very specific ways. Jesus said, "*If you abide in Me, and My words abide in you, ask whatever you wish, and it shall be done for you*" (JOHN 15:7 NASB). Realizing prayer actually worked, my faith increased.

I now found prayer to be a fantastic tool. Imagine asking God to give you the desire to do something! Once one has the desire, the problem is solved. The individual who has a bad habit would be much more effective in eliminating this habit if he would ask God to take his desire away. Once his desire is gone, the battle is won.

Faith has much in common with muscles. Without exercise, muscles atrophy and lose their strength. Exercise produces strong, flexible muscles. Muscles in good tone are less susceptible to injury. These principles are also true of faith. To keep our faith strong and resilient, we must exercise through prayer. God had some very important lessons to teach me in this area of exercising my faith through prayer. God, in His infinite wisdom, has chosen to bless us according to our faith. It is absolutely impossible to earn His favor on any other basis. In the book of Romans we find, "*To the man who does not work but trusts God who justifies the wicked, his faith is credited as righteousness*" (ROMANS 4:5). Earlier we saw that the author of Hebrews declares, "*Without faith it is impossible to please*

God..." **(HEBREWS 11:6)**. Paul carefully explains in Ephesians, "*For it is by grace you have been saved, through faith...not by works, so that no one can boast*" **(EPHESIANS 2:8-9)**.

In the early phases of my Christian experience, I thought God had really blown it by blessing man according to faith. My logical mind deduced man should be favored on the basis of achievement. However, as I experienced the love of Jesus Christ, the brilliance of God's method became apparent.

Jesus Christ was the only perfect man who ever lived. He was the visible expression of the invisible God. As Jesus Himself claimed, "*I and my Father are one. . . . Anyone who has seen Me has seen the Father*" **(JOHN 10:30, 14:9)**. Jesus is God. Therefore, what could I, a sinner, do to earn favor with God? Acts of sacrifice on my part would be as filthy rags compared to the price Jesus paid on the cross. In the gospel of John, the Pharisees asked Jesus how one could do the works of God. Jesus responded to this important question by saying, "*The work of God is this: to believe in the One He has sent*" **(JOHN 6:29)**. When I understood the only way I could do the works of God was by trusting Jesus Christ, I began to experience the power and joy of being a Christian. Performing for God or people was not necessary. As my faith in Jesus grew, acts of kindness, service, love, and sensitivity for my fellow man grew correspondingly.

In the remaining portion of this chapter, I want to share some of the experiences I encountered venturing out on the limb of faith. Many times, I found myself in predicaments where the only thing to do was pray. In every circumstance, God proved His faithfulness. Let's take off with an experience I had in Montana. The retreat director came to the microphone and began praying, "God, I know You really love these kids. You want them to have a wonderful time at this retreat. In the name of the Lord Jesus, I command this rain to stop and to ask You for sunshine. Amen."

Oh, no! I thought. What in the world is he doing? Doesn't he realize I have to speak next? We have enough problems at this camp. Susie, our two-month-old baby Jennifer, and I were participating in a Bible camp in Montana. We had 150 kids ranging from college age down to junior high. Many of the kids had serious problems. The pouring rain was not helping the situation.

These students had come from various cities throughout Montana and there were a few from Idaho. This was the largest group they had ever had. The committee in charge hoped to accomplish goals never realized in previous retreats. They wanted every student to make a personal decision for Jesus Christ, to grow in maturity and desire to share their faith with others.

WHY PRAY TO THE CEILING?

Susie and I had been assigned a difficult task. Our responsibilities were to show them how to receive Christ as their personal Savior, teach them how to be filled and controlled by the Holy Spirit, and teach them to share their faith by taking them witnessing door-to-door in a rural community.

The previous evening, I had shared my personal testimony. A number of the students had made decisions for Christ, but we still had many difficulties. We did not need to add to our problems by asking God for sunshine when big, black clouds were appearing overhead for miles in every direction.

After the director's prayer, I spoke on the ministry of the Holy Spirit. The presence of the Holy Spirit could be sensed throughout the campground. One of the counselors approached me after the message, with tears in her eyes. She told me she did not know Christ. Together we read God's promises in His Word. Within a half hour, she had a reason for living. Her radiance was proof that Christ had come into her life.

God continued working in people's lives, and the rain continued coming down in buckets! One teenager ran by the director, laughing and teasing about the rain. At about eleven thirty in the morning, the black clouds began to part, allowing us to see the sun. Warm sunshine became a reality. God had indeed answered prayer!

Each counselor had been told of our witnessing expedition, but we had not yet had time to meet together. Our meeting began at seven o'clock in the evening.t No sooner had I opened than one counselor vigorously refused to participate. Another refused to take his students, too. A minister began bombarding me with many unfair questions. Our problems loomed large, but if God was willing to change the weather, He certainly would help us lean to share our faith. God wanted this group to go witnessing. Many counselors, who before would not have taken a stand, were forced to share their convictions. Others voiced their desire to see the students step out in faith. We were going! But Satan was very busy hindering us in every way possible. There was still much opposition.

The meeting with the counselors lasted two hours. I had planned to use one of the hours to prepare for the evening message which followed. After the meeting, I had to go directly to the auditorium. There I found almost one hundred of the kids praying. They had been praying for over an hour. I had a hunch they were praying for our meeting with the counselors.

One of the unhappy counselors told me before I began speaking, "This idea of witnessing is a farce and it won't work," then he used the PA system to ask his students to meet immediately after the message. He was planning to take them home early on Sunday morning.

Before speaking, I asked God in the silence of my heart to perform a miracle. He led me to begin with these words: "I know this has been a wonderful experience for many of you this weekend. We have seen God bring us hot sunshine. We have seen lives changed. Tonight I am going to ask you to do something very difficult. I am asking you to come up to this microphone to tell what God has done in your life." As I spoke, I could see the disgust written on the face of one of the counselors. I stepped back from the microphone, hoping someone would have the courage to come forward. For one solid hour people came to share. I have never seen a more powerful demonstration of God's love.

A young teenager said, "I came here an atheist. A lady paid my way, and I came for a good time. She made a good investment because of the joy her dollars brought to my life in finding Jesus Christ." One of the counselors said, "I came here to help you kids, but I was the one who needed help!" He told what the Lord had done for him, then turned to his wife, with tears on his cheeks, and said, "Honey, I really love you." He had difficulty telling his wife privately that he loved her, but now told her in front of 150 people. Only God could make this possible. All the testimonies were from the heart, and the room was flooded with joy and happiness.

One of the students, being taken home next morning by the unhappy counselor, approached the microphone. He was a good student, an outstanding athlete, and commanded a great deal of respect. As he shared from a thankful heart, his counselor buried his face in his hands. God had reached him through a teenager, and he insisted on his group staying for the full weekend rather than returning early.

I closed by saying, "Nearly every one of you had expressed the thought that you do not want this retreat to be just a mountaintop experience. This will not happen if you learn to share your faith on a continuing basis. Tomorrow morning we are going into the community "like a mighty army' to share our faith in Jesus Christ. I would like those who want to be part of this army to stand." Over 140 people stood.

WHY PRAY TO THE CEILING?

I awoke early the next morning to bright, warm sunshine. The mountains were beautiful. Everyone was rushing around, preparing for the big event. By 11:00 a.m., we had eaten, had a training session, cleaned the camp, and driven sixty miles to begin witnessing.

Later, we met at the city park to share our experiences and have a picnic. The first to come was a counselor who had been outspoken against going. She related how the Lord had used her in leading a lady to Christ at the very first house she approached. An elderly blind man lived in the second home. He knew Christ, but was very lonely and very thankful for her visit.

Even the twelve-year-old campers had a great time. Twenty-five people received Christ in this small community because a group of teenagers was willing to trust God. As we headed home, everyone was thrilled. For many, this was not just a mountaintop experience. I heard later that many were taking advantage of opportunities to speak openly for Christ in the classroom.

When we were about five miles away from the park, rain began to fall; it fell steadily for the remaining days we were in Montana. When we boarded the plane to go back to California, it was snowing. God had answered many prayers. He had given us lots of fun and hot sunshine; He had changed lives; He had enabled us to overcome great opposition and to witness effectively; and He had sent many home with an enthusiasm about Himself that caused them to witness to their friends.

Two years later, I found myself in another difficult situation where prayer was the only reasonable course of action. This time our basketball team was in Vienna Del Mar, Chile. We were in the process of playing twenty games in twenty-six days in seven different countries. We were playing the best teams in Panama, Peru, Chile, Argentina, Brazil, Ecuador, and Colombia.

Vienna Del Mar was a beautiful resort city south of Santiago, but our situation was not pleasant. The previous evening we had lost 58-57 to an inferior team. Valpariso's tallest man had been smaller than our shortest man.

It seemed impossible for us to win. The referees were not fair; against Valpariso seven of our baskets had been disqualified—yet the Chilean Basketball Federation officials were furious because we were not winning. They said losing would hurt future crowds. Our interpreter told us we had better start winning or we would not be invited back to Chile.

The team met early the next morning to pray. All of us prayed hard. "God, help us to win. Give us the courage, determination, discipline, and strength to come back." Faith involves action as well as prayer. We ran up and down the hotel stairs for thirty minutes. The Chileans thought this was quite funny. This was humiliating, but good for us. We also cut down on our eating.

After an all-night train ride, we faced another team in Temuco, Chile. At half-time we led 29-27, but one of our players had fouled out of the game, and six others had four fouls each. Since our team was so much taller, the referees allowed our opponents to be very aggressive. At one time we had three of our players flat on the floor. It is nice to be 6'9", but it does little good if you have people climbing your back.

God not only allowed us to win by twenty points, but we finished the game without serious injuries. After the game, people rushed onto the floor to talk to the players about Jesus Christ. Two nights later, we defeated Chile's best team by eighteen points.

Athletes in Action went on to win fourteen of the last fifteen games, posting an impressive record of fifteen wins and five losses. Leading dignitaries and city officials approached us after the games to say, "Coach, this is the finest group of men we have ever seen from the United States. The thing we like most about your team is that they play like they speak during the half-time ceremonies." One man in Panama said, "I like your team because they live their religion on the basketball court."

As I look back over my coaching career, it is not the big wins over outstanding teams, not the beautiful sights we saw traveling that have made a lasting impression on my mind. My fondest memories come from those precious moments when Jesus Christ became real to someone, like one young Chilean, who invited Jesus into his life "with hospitality and love."

Prayer can be a fantastic tool for anyone, providing he is willing to apply the principles God has given regarding faith. D. L. Moody, the great evangelist of the nineteenth century, spent years crying out to God, "Give me more faith." But one day he read in ROMANS 10:17 NASB, "So faith comes from hearing, and hearing by the word of Christ."

In the daily devotional, Our Daily Bread, I remember reading, "Feed your faith on fact and let your doubts starve to death." My faith in Jesus Christ has grown immensely the past seven years, because I have been privileged to test

His claims in my daily living. I have seen and experienced the practicality of the Bible in prisons, juvenile detention homes, gymnasiums, college living groups, and public schools.

Show me an area of life where you are frustrated, guilty, or tense, and I will show you a biblical principle being broken. On the other hand, show me an area of your life where you are experiencing peace, harmony, and success, and I will show you a biblical principle you are following.

God has a rich, abundant life for each of us. All we need to do is ask Him and be obedient to His Word. I pray you will feed your faith on fact and let your doubts starve to death.

PROJECT 6

Write a five-minute presentation on why you believe Jesus Christ is the way, the truth, and the life. You may want to first read **Set Forth Your Case** by Clark Pinnock, **Know Why You Believe** by Paul Little, and **Jesus and the Intellectual** by Bill Bright. Take time to ground your faith in fact.

Begin to communicate with God in positive terms. Do not beg God. Confess sin and then claim His promise. Whenever we confess sin, we create a void that needs to be filled. If not filled with something positive, another negative fills it. Read the following verses and answer these questions:

Isaiah 26:3

Proverbs 15: 23

Philippians 4:6-7

Hebrews 11:6

1 John 1:9

What is the promise of the verse?

What condition must the believer make before experiencing blessing?

Are you experiencing the blessing?

Why is your answer yes or no? If no, meet the condition and experience His blessing.

Here are a few suggestions for successful prayer. Experiment with them.

First, establish a daily schedule of prayer. Time may vary from ten to thirty minutes. During this time meditate on the following;

- **(1) God loves me.** Praise Him for this love; quote Scripture and thank Him for sending Jesus.

- **(2) I love God.** Tell God of your love for Him.

- **(3) Claim these for your life:** GALATIANS 5:22-23 says, *"The fruit of the Spirit is love, joy, peace, patience, kindness, goodness, faithfulness, gentleness and self-control"*; and COLOSSIANS 2:9-10 NASB says, *"For in Him (Christ) all the fulness of deity dwells in bodily form, and in Him you have been made complete."* Christ has made us complete. We no longer have to beg for patience. We simply need to thank Jesus for patience.

- **(4) Pray for others.** Love others by praying for their needs. JOHN 13:35 says, *"By this shall all men know that ye are my disciples, if ye have love one for another."*

Second, meditate on scripture, especially the Psalms. Read the passage. After each verse, close your eyes and try to visualize what the passage says. For example, in PSALM 23:2-3 visualize yourself lying down in a green pasture beside a stream, enjoying peace and comfort.

Third, join a conversational prayer group. To get started, each person should write down a couple things he is thankful for and a couple things he needs. This helps those who are uncomfortable with group prayer, because it helps structure things a little. Now pray from the lists as the Spirit leads. Conversational prayer is a rare privilege.

Current Reflections

Two personal experiences, two prayers, two answers!

STORY ONE

One of my dysfunctions is waiting to refuel the gas tank until it is nearly empty. Mark Twain said, "If it weren't for the last minute, I wouldn't get anything done!" In my case, the decision was made to refuel the first thing in the morning. Departing Yakima in the wee hours one morning made it impossible to buy gas because the service stations were closed. No problem! I should be able to make it to Goldendale. However, soon my car and I were in the remotest parts of eastern Washington, and soon the needle on the gauge was on the left side of empty. Instead of looking for a gas station, my eyes were searching in vain for a farm!

My conversation with the Lord went something like this: "Lord, I know I don't deserve to be bailed out of this mess. It is totally my fault, but I would be so grateful if you would help me. I need to get to Portland. You know there isn't time to walk or hitchhike the twenty-plus miles to Goldendale." As the miles passed by, the anxiety level increased.

Suddenly, seemingly out of nowhere, an old camper truck with an even older Volkswagen bug appeared from the driver's side window. It had Alaska license plates. At 60 mph an immediate decision had to be made. Do I ask for gas? Or do I press on to Goldendale? I chose pressing on. Two miles down the highway, the needle on the gauge was even further left of the empty sign.

I remember saying, "You fool, go back, humble yourself. Ask for some gas, or you are going to be hoofing it."

Walking up to the camper with caution, I heard barking erupting from within the cabin. Timidly, I knocked on the door.

A male voice yelled: "What do you want?"

"Sorry to bother you, but I need some gas."

"Wait a minute."

Within seconds a small, wiry man came through the open door, pulling a shirt on with a big dog following.

"Need some gas, huh?" With a swipe of his arm, he grabbed a black hose tied to the side of the camper. "Wife won't be needing this." He was using his water hose to siphon gas. With a hard suck, the gas began to flow into his five-gallon can.

When I reached for my wallet, the man said, "Oh, no you don't! You aren't paying for this."

An opportunity to get to my billfold came. I had no money. A credit card wasn't going to help me either. I remembered several days earlier I had been given a check for $50. I found the check.

"Sir, I don't know how to tell you this. I spoke in Astoria, Oregon, the other day. When they paid me, I promised the Lord I would give it to someone in need. I had no idea you would be the person, but I really believe He wants me to give it to you."

"Mom, come out here quick! This man just gave me money!"

It turned out this couple left Alaska, looking for work. They had only $25 to their name. Now they had $75! Picture the scene: beside a deserted highway in eastern Washington, three people stood hugging each other.

STORY TWO

Three years ago, the day after Thanksgiving, I waited in my home for a call from my urologist. My prayer was to be cancer free—free from the worst swear word I know. It was a long wait. Finally, late in the day, the phone rang. Susie answered the phone. It was the doctor.

As I walked across the kitchen floor, I said to myself, "Lord, I am going to thank you regardless of the news."

The news: *"Fred, I am surprised to have to tell you two of your biopsies are malignant. You have prostate cancer."* I had the dreaded disease—the same enemy that ravaged my mother's body.

Fortunately, I no longer looked at life from purely a human perspective. No longer did I view life from a contract perspective: God loves me only when my prayers are answered the way I want. No longer did I believe in the *"prosperity gospel"*: good things happen to spiritual people, and bad things happen to bad people.

The journey through cancer has been one of the most valuable experiences of my life. Susie often said to me, *"If you live through cancer, you will never be the same."* In the past three years, the cancer experience has made it possible to be a tool of comfort, encouragement and hope for many men.

Summary

In the first story, I received exactly what I asked for—gas. I was given what I needed. In the second story, I did not receive what I wanted. I was given what I needed. No longer is it necessary for God to prove He loves me by giving me what I want. More often than not, the one who has the most special, wonderful relationship with God has had more difficulty in life.

Prayer has become the most beautiful language I speak. Prayer is a privilege to talk with the God of the universe through His Son Jesus Christ through the power of the Holy Spirit. At one time, this was very awkward for me—done in silence. Today these precious times of talking with God are even more precious when praying with my family and lovely friends. Listening to my nine-year-old granddaughter pray and then praying for her as we drive to school are the highlights of my day.

Chapter Notes

MEET MY
HEAD
COACH

10

NO LONGER A SLAVE

"

From the time I met Fred Crowell in 1997, I have been fascinated by him for many reasons, as well as simply drawn to him because of his personality and passion for life. I noticed very quickly that he was a genuine man who was bold in his faith and loved people. I remember thinking to myself, "I want to be like Fred Crowell when I grow up." This was an unconventional thought since I was already forty years old when I first met Fred.

Part of my interest in Fred and NBC Camps came from my own love of sports. I'll admit that I am a genuine sports nut. I sometimes stumble in remembering names of friends or colleagues; but ask me to name the starting lineup of the '66 Baltimore Orioles, and I'll rattle it off without hesitation. So, I've always dreamed of being able to make a living doing something associated with sports. When I met Fred Crowell, I found a man who had been able to make a living and raise a family by finding a vocation related to his love and passion for basketball. I admired that.

Beyond that, I love Jesus Christ. I gave my life to the Lord when I was eight years old. That was clearly the greatest decision I ever made in my life. So, when I saw a man who had been able to combine very successfully his passions for basketball and Jesus, I was in awe.

In Fred's own words, he said he was reluctant to commit his life to Jesus because he thought that would mean no more basketball. Somehow in our culture we believe that the "good life," the "fun life," exists outside of Christianity; we mistakenly believe a Christian has to follow a myriad of rules, not having any fun and sacrificing greatly in order to be worthy of Christ. Obviously, this is not true, but it is often believed. PSALM 37:4 says, *"Take delight in the Lord, and He will give you your heart's desires."* Note: more of our desires, not less. Take a look at what happened to Fred Crowell. He didn't get less basketball; he got more basketball...thirty-five years, over 167,000 lives touched through his company, NBC Camps. That's a lot of basketball!

When I was introduced to *Meet My Head Coach*, my first impression was to say, "Wow! This guy really means it when he talks about his faith and his love for Jesus Christ. He wrote a book about his faith and even put his real name on it!" He wasn't hiding behind some pseudonym. For me, the impact of the book was less about any specific chapter or topic, but more about seeing that Fred was bold enough to commit his faith to publishing it in a document for the ages. Reading the book simply solidified, for me, what I thought I saw in

NO LONGER A SLAVE

Fred Crowell—a man who was dedicated to Christ and his family, a man who had his priorities in the right order.

I have always struggled with having the right priorities in my life, having the right balance. It is very easy for me, as it is for many men, to wrap my own sense of worth around what I do for a living and become caught up in my work. In that context, it is difficult to find appropriate time for spiritual development, physical health, and being a loving, caring husband, as well as a responsible, available father. I have cherished watching Fred handle the balance in his life. I deeply respect and admire him as a business owner, husband and father. His influence on me has been immeasurable as I look to him as a mentor, advisor, role model, business colleague, brother in Christ and personal friend.

BRAD WILLIAMS

BRAD WILLIAMS LIVES IN REDDING, CALIFORNIA, WITH HIS WIFE, MARY KAY, AND THEY HAVE THREE SONS, MATTHEW, MICHAEL AND JONATHAN. BRAD GRADUATED FROM THE PENNSYLVANIA STATE UNIVERSITY WITH A B.S. IN CIVIL ENGINEERING AND FROM YORK COLLEGE OF PENNSYLVANIA WITH AN M.B.A. CURRENTLY, BRAD IS THE EXECUTIVE VICE PRESIDENT AT SIMPSON UNIVERSITY IN REDDING.

C oach, I will do anything to be able to play with the Athletes in Action team," said the strapping 6'8" athlete. Here was a coach's dream. Every good basketball team needs a big, strong center to congest the area near the basket and get the rebounds.

There did not seem to be any insurmountable problems to prevent this applicant from joining the team. His attitude was tremendous, he really loved the Lord, and he was a good basketball player. What more could a coach want? However, as I began to work with him, I realized a serious flaw in his character—no personal discipline!

Until directly involved in the lives of many with this problem, I never realized the devastating effect it can have on an individual. Most people regard athletes as highly disciplined. In my experience of nine years of competitive athletics and eight years of coaching, I have come to the conclusion that many athletes are poorly disciplined. The reason we believe they are highly disciplined is due to their excellence in a specific area.

There is no question that athletes must have tremendous determination, discipline, and drive to excel in their sport. However, a disciplined life involves more than discipline in one area. One of my former players was one of the most disciplined people I have ever seen. He would practice many hours a day, run with weight jackets, lift weights, and eat the correct food. But he was so lacking discipline in every other area as to be irresponsible.

Visit any major university during registration time. Coaches hire tutors, select the athlete's studies, direct him through registration, usually ahead of the other students, and pay the tuition fees. This does not imply athletes are not capable, because athletes generally get higher marks than the average student. It simply means athletes are babied. They are not forced to be responsible in areas outside of their specialization. Consequently many athletes have difficulty adjusting to the rigors of daily living. Marriage is often a difficult experience. Athletes often expect wives to serve them and cater to their every need.

I do not want to paint an unfavorable picture of athletes. I prefer working with men who have experienced athletic competition. People who have subjected themselves to demanding training schedules understand commitment. Properly challenged these men can excel in nearly anything they tackle. The fact that a well-trained athlete will never quit is perhaps his greatest asset.

I believe every individual would profit from belonging to a team committed to worthy goals, goals requiring dedication, sacrifice, and discipline. He would find few challenges too difficult.

As a coach I had to teach responsible behavior on and off the basketball court. While attempting to motivate and teach my players principles of successful living, I became aware of many inconsistencies in my own life. I never cease to marvel at my inability to recognize my own weaknesses. Instead of praying, "God, change the player," I began praying, "God, change their coach. Help me become a man of strong personal discipline."

A speaker was once asked how long it had taken him to prepare his message. His reply was, "All my life." I am finding that the development of personal discipline is a lifetime job. In some areas I have seen remarkable progress. In other areas I am improving slowly. Sometimes I wonder if I will ever completely succeed. Discipline and habit change are extremely difficult because they require faithfulness every day.

This may well be the most important chapter in the book because millions of Americans are enslaved to personal habits and do not have the discipline to overcome them. Our society is in serious difficulty due to the lack of willpower. Most men in the United States today are out of shape by the time they are twenty-two years old. The average American male past twenty cannot pass minimum physical stress tests. Thousands of people die each year of cigarette-induced lung cancer. Millions are slaves to alcohol and various drugs. The problem is obvious: inadequate and personal discipline. Most people simply do not have the intestinal fortitude to say no to their desires.

This problem has reached epidemic proportions. Thousands make lucrative incomes in the motivation industry. The libraries are full of books on this subject, and businesses sprout up every day attempting to help men and women succeed.

How can behavioral patterns deeply imbedded into the human personality be transformed? Is there an answer?

I believe we must turn to God for the dynamics of behavioral change. The thing that impresses me most about some of the outstanding men in this field is the fact that their basic principles have biblical origins.

Earl Nightengale relies heavily upon the principle of cause and effect. For every action, you will experience a corresponding reaction. The apostle Paul mentioned this same principle 2,000 years ago in his letter to the Galatians. Dale Carnegie taught the golden rule: Do unto others as you would have them do unto you. Jesus taught this principle and demonstrated it throughout His life. Norman Vincent Peale repeatedly gives God the credit in his writings; and Dr. Maltz says that one's self-image is changed, for better or for worse, not by his intellect or by intellectual knowledge alone, but by experience. This is precisely what Jesus taught when He said, "You must be born again." Another version of the Bible explains Paul's words like this: *"When someone becomes a Christian he becomes a brand new person inside. He is not the same any more. A new life has begun"* (2 CORINTHIANS 5:17 TLB).

In other words, Jesus was saying that in order to experience power, the old nature must die. Once we have received Christ, we have a new nature. Thus we can begin to experience God's power. Unfortunately, many Christians do not see habits changed because they do not know how to allow God to change their lives.

In the remainder of this chapter, I shall discuss two distinct methods of changing bad habits. I am sure everyone has tried the first method. When trying to eliminate a deeply imbedded personal habit such as smoking, drinking, swearing, biting fingernails, gossiping, and complaining, there are many techniques to use. The most common is the life-force method. "By the sheer determination of my will I can overcome this ugly habit." This method is widely practiced at New Year's and other special occasions. This technique is excellent if your willpower is stronger than the habit. Unfortunately, this is seldom the case.

I recall visiting a loved one in a hospital. He was recovering from his third bout of pneumonia. His body ached from the chronic bronchial infection caused by cigarettes. The doctor sternly warned him that his cigarette habit could be fatal. My friend vowed he had smoked his last cigarette. He was finished. He even went through a stop smoking course which was essentially a scare session. In spite of his good intentions, cigarettes won.

The life-force method is unsuccessful because it violates biblical principles as well as psychological principles. Dr. Maltz says, "It has been amply demonstrated that attempting to use effort or will power to change beliefs or cure bad habits has an adverse rather than a beneficial effect."

The second method is the technique used by nearly every leader in the field of positive thinking. Each expresses his philosophy uniquely to fit his program, but in reality all of these leaders come to the same conclusions. Basically they are saying, "Establish a goal, picture the goal in your mind, imagine it actually happening, and in time you will achieve the desired objective."

Positive thinking is a wonderful concept and even more effective when you rely totally on God. I call this the faith-rest method. "By faith, I will rest in the promises of God, trusting Him to transform my life." Now we must consider how to rely upon God to solve deeply imbedded personal habits. Once people realize the simplicity of God's method, they are eager to apply His principles. *"Therefore, I urge you, brothers, in view of God's mercy, to offer your bodies as living sacrifices, holy and pleasing to God--this is your spiritual act of worship. Do not conform any longer to the pattern of this world, but be transformed by the renewing of your mind. Then you will be able to test and approve what God's will is--His good, pleasing and perfect will"* (ROMANS 12:1-2).

STEPS TO A TRANSFORMED LIFE

KNOW THE TRUTH ABOUT YOURSELF

The aim of self-image psychology is not to create a fictitious self which is all-powerful, arrogant, egotistic, all-important. Such an image is as inappropriate and unrealistic as the inferior image of self. Our aim is to find the "real self." . . . It is common knowledge among psychologists that most of us underrate ourselves; shortchange ourselves and sell ourselves short. Actually, there is no such thing as "superiority complex." People who seem to have one are actually suffering from feelings of inferiority—their "superior" self is a fiction, a cover-up to hide from themselves and others their deep-down feelings of inferiority and insecurity.

How can you know the truth about yourself? How can you make a true evaluation? It seems to me that here psychology must turn to religion. The Scriptures tell us that God created man a little lower than the angels and gave him dominion; that God created man in His own image.

I wholeheartedly agree with Dr. Maltz, that to know the truth about self we must turn to the Bible. It is absolutely essential to understand God's view of man to change effectively personal habits. To change behavior, the self-image must be changed. Once we begin to comprehend God's love for us, His unconditional acceptance, and His desire to transform our lives, we can begin having confidence that the ugliness in our lives can be changed.

Dr. Maltz quotes Thomas Carlyle as saying, "Alas! The fearful unbelief is unbelief in yourself!" Dr. Maltz says, "Of all the traps and pitfalls in life, a self-disesteem is the deadliest, the hardest to overcome; for it is the pit designed and dug by our own hands, summed up in the phrase, 'It's no use, I can't do it!'"

God says you can overcome this trap of self-destruction by experiencing the love of His Son. God knows the only way to change the self-image of man is through experiencing success. The self-image is changed the same way it was made—through experience. If you want to change your self-image, I suggest you begin by experiencing Jesus Christ and establishing God's Word as your absolute authority.

It is only logical that if our greatest need is love and God is love, then we can best meet our need by coming to Him. *"God is love. Whoever lives in love lives in God, and God in him. In this way, love is made complete among us so that we will have confidence on the day of judgment, because in this world we are like Him"* (1 JOHN 4:16-17).

RECOGNIZE THE HABIT AS SIN

Sin can be defined as anything that separates us from God. It can be characterized by an attitude of active rebellion or passive indifference. When discussing sin, we must be careful not to imply certain acts are sin for everyone. Unfortunately, many people judge another's spirituality on the basis of external habits. However, God looks on the inner qualities of man.

Sin is the name for those things in a life which cause barriers between the individual and God. We would be more effective in our witness if we refrained from telling others the things they need to clean up in their lives. Let God do this. He does a far more effective job.

With this caution in mind, I hope I can make reference to specific acts without suggesting these are universal sins. They are only sins if they bug you, hinder your relationship with others or hinder your relationship with God.

A good friend of mine decided he wanted to quit smoking. He had tried unsuccessfully many times, but had recently taken the first step in overcoming his habit by experiencing the reality of Jesus Christ as his personal Savior. Even though many of his friends wanted to suggest he give up the cigarettes since he suffered severely from asthma, none said a word. The man had to recognize the habit in his life as sin before he could experience success. One day he approached me to say, "Fred, I know now God wants me to quit smoking because it is ruining my health." Now, he was heading for step three.

Before we discuss step three, I want to give you another example of this principle. A Christian was having problems with a bad habit. It was not bothering anyone else, but it was a stumbling block to his own personal growth. He bit his nails to the point of drawing blood. It bothered him that he could not eliminate this habit. He was embarrassed to allow others to see his nails. Eventually, he recognized this habit as sin because it prevented him from experiencing God's power completely. This was a very important step. Now God could begin to transform his desires.

CONFESS THE HABIT AS SIN

After recognizing the habit as sin, it is important to verbalize this sin to God, seeking His forgiveness. In 1 JOHN 1:9 we read, *"If we confess our sins, He is faithful and just and will forgive us our sins..."*

Not only must we confess our sins, but we must believe that we are forgiven. *"This is the confidence we have in approaching God: that if we ask anything according to His will, He hears us. And If we know that He hears us--whatever we ask--we know that we have what we asked of Him"* (1 JOHN 5:14-15). Certainly it is God's will for us to overcome ugly habits in our lives which prevent us from realizing our full potential.

One day my friend prayed, "God, I realize it is sin for me to smoke cigarettes. Thank You for forgiving me and removing my desire to smoke. Amen."

It is important to realize at this point that God works uniquely in each person's life. Some experience immediate transformation, while others battle indefinitely. In the case of my friend who had smoked heavily for many years, he stopped smoking completely in a few weeks. God gave him the power to accomplish a feat he could never have accomplished through his own discipline.

The principles involved in confessions have much in common with a baby learning to walk. A baby does not learn to walk immediately. He kicks, rolls over, crawls, stands, falls, stands again, takes a step, and falls again, until one day he walks across the room and dives into his parents' waiting arms. Eventually walking is second nature. Once in awhile, he still falls, but he immediately gets up.

Unfortunately, many Christians do not understand these same principles apply to confession of sin. When we fall in sin, we confess that sin, experience God's forgiveness, and move ahead. As we initially ask God to transform bad habits, we are much like the baby learning to walk. We fall. The thing we must not do is continue lying down. We get up by confessing our sins.

The nail-biter began this experiment by confessing his sin. Several hours later, he was deeply engrossed in some activity. Suddenly he realized his fingers were in his mouth. Abruptly he jerked hem out, "Oh, no!" then, "God, please forgive me for biting my nails." Here is a perfect example of awakening conscience. Soon he was going a full day without biting his nails, then several days, and finally weeks. Each time he failed, he was quick to confess his sin.

THANK GOD FOR FORGIVING YOU BY ACTING FORGIVEN

One of the hardest things to change is self-pity. Often I have seen people fail, then cry out to God, "How could You let me do it?" God had nothing to do with it. The person sinned. *"When tempted, no one should say, 'God is tempting me."* (JAMES 1:13).

It is possible to seek forgiveness, but not accomplish any good because there was not complete repentance. God forgives on one condition. This condition is faith. *"Now faith is being sure of what we hope for and certain of what we do not see"* (HEBREWS 11:1). Therefore, when I ask God to forgive me, I must be prepared to believe that I have been forgiven. My slate is clean.

I believe God wants us to put our faith on the line. Either God's Word is real, or He is not telling the truth. The biggest fool of all is the one who says he believes God but denies Him in daily living. God's promises must grip our lives daily as we attempt to live successfully in a "hell-like world."

I would like you to join me in a lifetime commitment. Let's see how many of God's promises we can make real in our lives before we meet Him face to face.

PROJECT 7

Name the four steps involved in the faith-rest method.

1.

2.

3.

4.

Carefully select one specific habit you would like to break and begin applying the faith –rest method daily as the need occurs. Remember your responsibility is to apply the method, and God will be faithful to do the changing.

Listed below are some suggestions for strengthening personal discipline in your life. Before embarking on any of the following, establish personal goals and a well-defined program to follow.

Exercise. Get involved with jogging, aerobics, swimming, etc. Exercise will relieve tension and give you more energy. Before beginning, make sure you have had a recent physical and follow an approved program of exercise.

Memorizing the Bible is excellent for mental discipline. I CORINTHIANS 14:40 AND 2 CORINTHIANS 4:2 teach us the importance of a disciplined life.

Fasting has tremendous value in building personal discipline. The hunger drive is extremely strong. If you can say no to food, you can say no to nearly any temptation. Before fasting, you should study fasting from the Scripture and other sources. *God's Chosen Fast* by Arthur Wallis is an excellent book, and health food stores also have literature on the subject.

Current Reflections

Everything I said in this chapter is true. Yet there was something I didn't know thirty-three years ago: it is not easy to be no longer a slave. I know this only too well. I am still a slave to some of the self-discipline issues I faced in my late twenties. I am still selfish. I still lack self-discipline in many areas. I still get angry too quickly.

What I now know is that it takes as much as three to five years of consistent dedication and work to make character changes. It doesn't just happen. Furthermore, no addiction ever goes away. Addictions can be either good or bad. For instance, lifting weights, jogging, and reading good books are good addictions; but, out of balance, they can become bad addictions. In addition, no one is immune from addiction; we all have them.

I have also learned the bad ones are like the alligator in the swamp. Did you know an alligator can live for six months without eating? Then in one day, they can devour an entire zebra. Likewise, addictions can be silent for years, and then one day rise up and bite.

Wearing orthodontic braces these past two years has given me a completely new perspective on change. People hate change, partly because it causes stress and creates imbalance. We are habit-forming creatures. We want to live in homeostasis. My wise orthodontist began my treatment with a very thin wire. He wanted to tell my teeth gently to wake up and get ready for a move. They could have been moved in half the time but at a great expense to my personal comfort and total distress to my mind and body. It took two years of gentle persuasion to move my teeth into the desired location.

With the braces off and treatment finished, I now have a new problem. My teeth want to return to their crooked positions; they want to go home. Daily, the teeth must be encouraged to stay in their new home.

Similar to orthodontia, if you sincerely want to change, you must be willing to work on the changes you desire the remaining days of your life. Know it will not be easy, but know, also, it will be worth it. Mark Twain was correct when he said, "You cannot break a bad habit by throwing it out the window. You've got to walk it slowly (and deliberately) down the stairs." To use Mark Twain's example, it takes many steps, and much commitment, to get to the door. The relentless pursuit of excellence is the difference between those who live well and those who live poorly.

Chapter Notes

11

GET IN THE GAME

"

It was a sunny Sunday morning in July, a day I will never forget. My family and I packed the van and headed towards Medical Lake, Washington, to my very first NBC Camp. I was nine. As we drove down the long dirt road into camp, I remember feeling very nervous. I saw the lake, some outdoor courts, and several other buildings. My mom was the first to exit the van and, typical of moms, had all my paperwork in hand. After we had registered, my dad and I walked over to a row of five small cabins, chose one, and set down my suitcase and sleeping bag. Next we unpacked my hoop shoes and basketball and headed over to a very large metal field house. Inside, we were overwhelmed by two large basketball courts and hoops that seemed to be everywhere! Already there were lots of other kids, some big and some small, shooting at the open baskets. My dad nodded in approval. So we walked back outside and found my mom and little brother to accompany us back to the van. I knew the time had come. Teary-eyed, I said goodbye and watched my family drive away. I wouldn't see them again until the next Saturday.

The first two days of camp were incredibly hard for me. I worked harder than I had ever worked in my little nine-year-old life. I found myself really missing home until Wednesday. Then something inside of me clicked, and I realized. . . I loved it here! Every evening we heard powerful talks from a man by the name of Fred Crowell. I felt myself changing every time he spoke. Not only was I learning how to be a better basketball player but, more importantly, I was learning how to become a better person, son, and follower of Jesus Christ. Saturday finally came, and I had never been so glad to see my parents and even my little brother! I was excited to go home and practice all I had learned. Little did I know what God had in store for me over the next thirty summers.

Summer after summer, I returned to NBC Camps. I not only attended as a camper, but I was able to work as a junior counselor and be a part of the kitchen crew to help finance my way to camp. At age thirteen, I re-dedicated my life to Jesus Christ at camp. At age seventeen, I was chosen for the NBC Camps Australian tour team, an experience that greatly impacted my teenage life. My next four summers were spent in several positions at NBC Camps: coach, master teacher and mid-school instructor, evening program coordinator, and tours coach and team member.

However, my first big management job for NBC Camps was assigned to me by Fred Crowell himself. He asked me to be "Manager of the Field House."

I remember spending hours cleaning at night, keeping the field house gyms spotless, and making sure no litter was to be found anywhere! Next Fred asked me to become a site director at Upper Columbia Academy in Spangle, Washington, for four years. Then expansion led to opening a campsite in western Washington, at Auburn Adventist Academy, where I have been privileged to now direct for thirteen seasons. In the year 2000, Fred Crowell promoted me to be one of his vice presidents.

My life is a direct result of Fred Crowell's listening to God and putting his faith into action to create the ministry of NBC Camps. *Meet My Head Coach* will give you insight into how to follow Christ in a real way. It will take you on the journey of a man who once did not believe in the power of Christ, and then it will show you how God softened his heart so He could use him as a tool to impact thousands of young people's lives, just like mine.

ROGER A. SMITH

ROGER SMITH AND HIS BEAUTIFUL WIFE, JESSE, MAKE THEIR HOME IN PUYALLUP, WASHINGTON, WHERE HE HAS BEEN TEACHING SCHOOL FOR SIXTEEN YEARS. ROGER HOLDS A DOUBLE MAJOR IN ELEMENTARY AND SPECIAL EDUCATION FROM PACIFIC LUTHERAN UNIVERSITY AND A MASTER'S DEGREE FROM GONZAGA UNIVERSITY. HIS ENERGY, ENTHUSIASM, EXPERIENCE, AND COMMITMENT TO EXCELLENCE ARE VALUABLE ASSETS AS AN NBC CAMPS VICE PRESIDENT.

Our lives are so short and there is so much to be done with them. We all tend to say, "If only I had more time." It really is not a matter of more time but, rather, effective use of the time entrusted to us. Voltaire was once asked how he would live if he had twenty-four hours left. His reply was, "One minute at a time."

The major issue is living a life pleasing to our Savior. In a world full of hypocrisy, lying, stealing, and violence, people are starved for love and acceptance. The greatest thing that ever happened to me was meeting Jesus Christ. The greatest thing I can do for another is to introduce him to Christ. Jesus said, *"For what does it profit a man to gain the whole world and forfeit his soul?"* **(MARK 8:36 NASB)**. Unfortunately, Christians have been unwilling to share this life-changing message because we fear rejection.

Knowing that people want to be accepted and loved, we need not fear sharing Christ with them. After all, Christ is love **(1 JOHN 4:8)**. Talking about Christ can be natural because He is the attractive one. Most people have not rejected Jesus, only those who have followed Him. Too many of us are concerned about judging another man's external behavior. I am so thankful God has called me to love people and not judge them.

When people realize we love them and do not wish to criticize their behavior, invariably they begin to accept our friendship and allow us to influence their lives. To have a significant impact upon another life, we must live what we encourage others to do. All too often we are forced to say, "Don't do as I do, do as I say." To paraphrase Jesus, before you tell your brother to get the twig out of his eye, remove the two-by-four from your own eye. First, live a lifestyle that is attractive to others; then learn to talk intelligently about your faith in Christ. Peter instructs believers in **1 PETER 3:15**, *"Always be prepared to give an answer to everyone who asks you to give the reason for the hope that you have. But do this with gentleness and respect."*

In counseling others, I find confidence and security in the Bible. *"All Scripture is inspired by God and profitable for teaching, for reproof, for correction, for training in righteousness; that the man of God may be adequate, equipped for every good work"* **(2 TIMOTHY 3:16-17 NASB)**. If men want to lead happy, profitable, fulfilling lives, they must follow biblical principles.

I have come to the conclusion that if the Bible commanded me to jump through a brick wall, I would do it because I know it is my responsibility to be obedient and God's responsibility to get me through the wall. However, I am grateful

God does not ask me to do nonsensical things like jumping through brick walls. The real test of obedience comes when He commands me to do things that I do not want to do at the moment.

Once we are willing to be obedient to God's Word, we will begin to have a positive influence in others' lives. Our happiness and joy will radiate to others. We can begin to answer their questions confidently and intelligently.

Many ask, "Don't you feel in a box or mold doing exactly what God tells you to do? How can you be true to your real self?"

The answer lies in the meaning of freedom. I have complete freedom in Christ. Freedom is the length of rope between you and the stake. Once we learn to operate within the length of rope given us, we have freedom. The most frustrated young people are those searching for boundary lines, but finding none.

Obeying the Bible is like driving on the freeway versus driving across fields. My wife and I often drive to Coeur d'Alene, Idaho, thirty minutes from our home via freeway. When driving the freeway, we have many privileges removed: we must drive a specified speed, travel in the right lane except when passing, and follow numerous other rules. If we disobey, we will probably receive a ticket from a state patrolman. We are not obligated to travel on the freeway, however. We could go through the backwoods and do as we please, but this thirty-minute trip on a smooth road could end up being an all-day affair through the fields. Therefore, we are perfectly willing to follow the freeway rules which enhance our safety and make it possible to reach our destination quickly.

How can we be responsible and yet be our real selves? The answer lies in first understanding the true meaning of freedom and then in realizing we really do not want to be "our real selves."

I said this to a young woman who had spent nearly two thousand dollars in psychotherapy trying to find her true self. She was shocked when I told her I didn't want to follow my true self. The wheels began to turn as we discussed the fact that man is innately evil. Being the mother of three, she could identify with the selfishness and cruelty our children exercise instinctively. I know what I am, and I do not want to be that way. I want to be like Christ, whom I was originally created to be like. The more I allow Him to control my life, the more attractive I will be.

Are you willing to follow Jesus Christ and His Word? Before you say yes, realize He makes some demanding claims on your life. For example, He says young people must obey their parents. The Bible does not say if your parents are right or even nice you obey them; it simply says obey! For you young men who like to wear your hair long, the Word of God says to get your head shaved, if your parents tell you to do so. This is what obey may mean for you.

Girls, the Bible gives explicit instructions regarding dating and marriage. Are you willing to obey them, or will you bend the rules to suit your fancy? I see many women who violated the tremendous principles God has given for successful homes because they thought they could change the young man. I tell girls that they should not even date those who do not love our Lord. I realize those are rigid words, but I believe in them because of the heartache I see daily.

Wives, God is all in favor of freedom and liberation. He provides this for everyone. We find our freedom by obeying Him. One of your specific responsibilities is to yield final authority in the home to your husband and respect him. For the woman who has not selected a husband who sincerely desires to be like Christ, this principle is very, very difficult to follow, but nonetheless imperative.

Husbands, are you willing to call anger and temper sin, admit it when you are wrong by asking forgiveness of those you hurt? We are to be leaders in our homes. This involves leadership with love. The husband sets the pace. What better way than telling other members of the family of our love for them. Leadership without love is dictatorship, and love without leadership is to be a marshmallow.

I remember my coaching debut at the University of Alaska. Thirty-six young men attended our first meeting. Each of these collegians had great aspirations. They looked around the room, sizing up the competition. It surprised them when I said I would not cut a man. Each was welcome to be a member of the team for the entire season. Ability was not a factor. Willingness and obedience would be my only requirements.

The rules were not complicated. I expected each athlete to attend class and maintain at least a C average. Drinking, smoking, and late hours were not acceptable. I assured them I was not going to be a policeman. We would operate on the honor system. If they could not live up to these standards, then they should play intramural basketball. We finished the season with thirteen men on the squad. We won thirteen games and lost three; it was the first winning season in the history of the school. The grade point average of the team was a B, and a number of the people were class officers and student leaders. I never cut a man. Some quit because practice was too tough, others failed academically, and several came to inform me they were not willing to give up cigarettes or alcohol. I shall never forget that wonderful basketball team. It won games it had no business winning, against superior opponents. The men had two qualities so many lack—willingness and obedience.

Jesus Christ is the Christian's head coach. He is not going to cut anyone who goes out for the team. We can be part of His team as long as we are willing and obedient to His Word. He does not punish our lack of perfection. He keeps loving us just as we are. He does not need our ability; He only wants our availability.

I have played sports for many excellent coaches, but Jesus Christ is the only one worthy of the title Head Coach. In the years, months, days, and minutes that you and I have left, shall we show others the reality of Christ through our own lives?

By the way, have you met my Head Coach?

Chapter Notes

MEET MY HEAD COACH

APPENDIX 1

Appendix 1

HAVE YOU HEARD OF THE FOUR SPIRITUAL LAWS?

Just as there are physical laws that govern the physical universe, so are there spiritual laws which govern your relationship with God

LAW ONE

GOD LOVES YOU, AND HAS A WONDERFUL PLAN FOR YOUR LIFE.

(REFERENCES CONTAINED IN THIS BOOKLET SHOULD BE READ IN CONTEXT FROM THE BIBLE WHEREVER POSSIBLE.)

GOD'S LOVE

"For God so loved the world, that He gave His only begotten Son, that whoever believes in Him should not perish, but have eternal life" (JOHN 3:16).

GOD'S PLAN

(Christ speaking) *"I came that they might have life, and might have it abundantly"* (that it might be full and meaningful) (JOHN 10:10).

Why is it that most people are not experiencing the abundant life?

LAW TWO

MAN IS SINFUL **AND** SEPARATED **FROM GOD, AND THUS HE CANNOT KNOW AND EXPERIENCE GOD'S LOVE AND PLAN FOR HIS LIFE.**

MAN IS SINFUL

"For all have sinned and fall short of the glory of God" (ROMANS 3:23).

Man was created to have fellowship with God; but, because of his own stubborn self-will, he chose to go his own independent way and fellowship with God was broken. This self-will, characterized by an attitude of active rebellion or passive indifference, is an evidence of what the Bible calls sin.

MAN IS SEPARATED

"For the wages of sin is death" (spiritual separation from God) **(ROMANS 6:23)**.

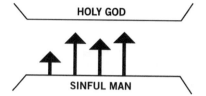

God is holy and man is sinful.

A great chasm separates the two.

Man is continually trying to reach God and the abundant life through his own efforts: good life, ethics, philosophy, SINFUL MAN etc.

The third Law gives us the only answer to this dilemma. . .

LAW THREE

JESUS CHRIST IS GOD'S ONLY **PROVISION FOR MAN'S SIN. THROUGH** HIM **YOU CAN KNOW AND EXPERIENCE GOD'S LOVE AND PLAN FOR YOUR LIFE.**

HE DIED IN OUR PLACE

"But God demonstrates His own love toward us, in that while we were yet sinners, Christ died for us." **(ROMANS 5:8)**.

HE ROSE FROM THE DEAD

"Christ died for our sins . . . He was buried . . . He was raised on the third day according to the Scriptures . . . He appeared to Cephas, then to the twelve. After that He appeared to more than five hundred . . ." **(I CORINTHIANS 15:3-6)**.

HE IS THE ONLY WAY

"Jesus said to him, 'I am the way, and the truth, and the life; no one comes to the Father, but through Me'" **(JOHN 14:6)**.

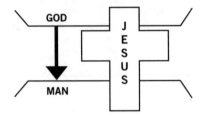

God has bridged the chasm which separates us from Him by sending His Son, Jesus Christ, to die on the cross in our place.

It is not enough just to know these three laws . . .

LAW FOUR

WE MUST INDIVIDUALLY RECEIVE **JESUS CHRIST AS OUR SAVIOR AND LORD; THEN WE CAN KNOW AND EXPERIENCE GOD'S LOVE AND PLAN FOR OUR LIVES.**

WE MUST RECEIVE CHRIST

"But as many as received Him, to them He gave the right to become children of God, even to those who believe in His name" (JOHN 1:12).

WE RECEIVE CHRIST THOUGH FAITH

"For by grace you have been saved through faith; and that not of yourselves, it is the gift of God; not as a result of works, that no one should boast" (EPHESIANS 2:8, 9).

WE RECEIVE CHRIST BY PERSONAL INVITATION

(Christ is speaking): *"Behold, I stand at the door and knock: if anyone hears My voice and opens the door, I will come in to him"* (REVELATION 3:20).

Receiving Christ involves turning to God from self, trusting Christ to come into our lives, to forgive our sins and to make us what He wants us to be. It is not enough to give intellectual assent to His claims or to have an emotional experience.

These two circles represent two kinds of lives:

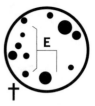

SELF-CONTROLLED LIFE

E—Ego or finite self on the throne

+—Christ outside the life

•—Interests controlled by self, often resulting
in discord and frustration

CHRIST-CONTROLLED LIFE

+—Christ on the throne of the life

E—Ego—self dethroned

•—Interests under control of infinite God,
resulting in harmony with God's plan

Which circle represents your life?

Which circle would you like to have represent your life?

The following explains how you can receive Christ:

YOU CAN RECEIVE CHRIST RIGHT NOW THROUGH PRAYER

(prayer is talking with God)

God knows your heart and is not so concerned with your words as He is with
the attitude of your heart. The following is a suggested prayer:

**"Lord Jesus, I need You. I open the door of my life and receive You as
my Savior and Lord. Thank You for forgiving my sins. Take control of
the throne of my life. Make me the kind of person You want me to be."**

Does this prayer express the desire of your heart? If it does, pray this prayer
right now, and Christ will come into your life, as He promised.

HOW TO KNOW THAT CHRIST IS IN YOUR LIFE

Did you receive Christ into your life? According to His promise in REVELATION
3:20, where is Christ right now in relation to you? Christ said that He would
come into your life. Would He mislead you? On what authority do you know

that God has answered your prayer? (Answer: the trustworthiness of God Himself and His Word).

THE BIBLE PROMISES ETERNAL LIFE TO ALL WHO RECEIVE CHRIST

"And the witness is this, that God has given us eternal life, and this life is in His Son. He who has Son has the life; he who does not have the Son of God does not have the life. These things I have written to you who believe in the name of the Son of God, in order that you may know that you have eternal life" **(1 JOHN 5:11-13).**

Thank God often that Christ is in your life and that He will never leave you **(HEBREWS 13:5).** You can know that the living Christ dwells in you, and that you have eternal life, from the very moment you invite Him in on the basis of His promise. He will not deceive you.

What about feelings?

DO NOT DEPEND UPON FEELINGS

The promise of God's Word, not our feelings, is our authority. The Christian lives by faith (trust) in the trustworthiness of God himself and His Word. This train diagram illustrates the relationship between fact (God and His Word), faith (our trust in God and His Word), and feeling (the result of our faith and obedience) **(JOHN 14:21).**

The train will run with or without the caboose. However, it would be futile to attempt to pull the train by the caboose. In the same way, we as Christians do not depend on feelings or emotions, but place our faith (trust) in the trustworthiness of God and the promises of His Word.

NOW THAT YOU HAVE RECEIVED CHRIST

The moment that you, as an act of faith, received Christ, many things happened, including the following:

Christ came into your life **(REVELATION 3:20 AND COLOSSIANS 1:27).**

Your sins were forgiven **(COLOSSIANS 1:14).**

You became a child of God **(JOHN 1:12).**

You began the great adventure for which God created you (JOHN 10:10; 2 CORINTHIANS 5:17 AND 1 THESSALONIANS 5:18).

Can you think of anything more wonderful that could happen to you than receiving Christ? Would you like to thank God in prayer right now for what He has done for you? The very act of thanking God demonstrates faith.

Now what?

SUGGESTIONS FOR CHRISTIAN GROWTH

Spiritual growth results from trusting Jesus Christ. *"The righteous man shall live by faith"* (GALATIANS 3: 11). A life of faith will enable you to trust God increasingly with every detail of your life, and to practice the following:

G   Go to God in prayer daily (JOHN 15:7).

R   Read God's Word daily (ACTS 17:11)—begin with the Gospel of John.

O   Obey God, moment by moment (JOHN 14:21).

W   Witness for Christ by your life and words (MATTHEW 4:19; JOHN 15:8).

T   Trust God for every detail of your life (1 PETER 5:7).

H   Holy Spirit—allow Him to control and empower your daily life and witness (GALATIANS 5:16, 17; ACTS 1:8).

THE IMPORTANCE OF A GOOD CHURCH

In HEBREWS 10:25, we are admonished to forsake not *"the assembling of ourselves together...."* Several logs burn brightly together, but put one aside on the cold hearth and the fire goes out. So it is with your relationship to other Christians. If you do not belong to a church, do not wait to be invited. Take the initiative; call the pastor of a nearby church where Christ is honored and His Word is preached. Start this week and make plans to attend regularly.

MEET MY HEAD COACH

APPENDIX 2

Appendix 2

HAVE YOU MADE THE WONDERFUL DISCOVERY OF THE SPIRIT-FILLED LIFE?

EVERY DAY CAN BE AN EXCITING ADVENTURE FOR THE CHRISTIAN who knows the reality of being filled with the Holy Spirit and who lives constantly, moment by moment, under His gracious control.

The Bible tells us that there are three kinds of people:

NATURAL MAN

(One who has not received Christ) *"But a natural man does not accept the things of the Spirit of God; for they are foolishness to him, and he cannot understand them, because they are spiritually appraised"* (1 CORINTHIANS 2:14).

SELF-CONTROLLED LIFE

E—Ego or finite self on the throne

+—Christ outside the life

•—Interests controlled by self, often resulting in discord and frustration

SPIRITUAL MAN

(One who is controlled and empowered by the Holy Spirit)

"But he who is spiritual appraises all things. . ." (1 CORINTHIANS 2:15).

CHRIST-CONTROLLED LIFE

+—Christ on the throne of the life

E—Ego—self dethroned

•—Interests under control of infinite God, resulting in harmony with God's plan

CARNAL MAN

(One who has received Christ, but who lives in defeat because he trusts in his own efforts to live the Christian life)

SELF-CONTROLLED LIFE

E—Ego or finite self on the throne

+—Christ dethroned

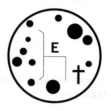

•—Interests controlled by self, often resulting in discord and frustration

"And I, brethren, could not speak to you as to spiritual men, but as to carnal men, as to babes in Christ. I gave you milk to drink, not solid food; for you were not yet able to receive it. Indeed, even now you are not yet able, for you are still carnal (self-controlled, fleshly). For since there is jealousy and strife among you, are you not fleshly, and are you not walking like mere men?" (1 CORINTHIANS 3:1-3).

GOD HAS PROVIDED FOR US AN ABUNDANT AND FRUITFUL CHRISTIAN LIFE.

Jesus said, *"I came that they might have life, and might have it abundantly"* (JOHN 10:10).

"I am the vine, you are the branches; he who abides in Me and I in him, he bears much fruit; for apart from Me you can do nothing" (JOHN 15:5).

"But the fruit of the Spirit is love, joy, peace, patience, kindness, goodness, faithfulness, gentleness, self-control; against such things there is no law" (GALATIANS 5:22, 23).

"But you shall receive power when the Holy Spirit has come upon you; and you shall be My witnesses both in Jerusalem, and in all Judea and Samaria, and even to the remotest part of the earth" (ACTS 1:8).

THE SPIRITUAL MAN—Some personal traits which result from trusting God:

CHRIST-CENTERED	**LOVE**
EMPOWERED BY THE HOLY SPIRIT	**JOY**
INTRODUCES OTHERS TO CHRIST	**PEACE**
EFFECTIVE PRAYER LIFE	**PATIENCE**
UNDERSTANDS GOD'S WORD	**KINDNESS**
TRUSTS GOD	**FAITHFULNESS**
OBEYS GOD	**GOODNESS**

The degree to which these traits are manifested in the life depends upon the extent to which the Christian trusts the Lord with every detail of his life, and upon his maturity in Christ. One who is only beginning to understand the ministry of the Holy Spirit should not be discouraged if he is not as fruitful as more mature Christians who have known and experienced this truth for a longer period.

Why is it that most Christians are not experiencing the abundant life?

CARNAL CHRISTIANS CANNOT EXPERIENCE THE ABUNDANT AND FRUITFUL CHRISTIAN LIFE.

The carnal man trusts in his own efforts to live the Christian life:

He is either uninformed about, or has forgotten, God's love, forgiveness, and power (ROMANS 5:8-10; HEBREWS 10:1-25; 1 JOHN 1; 2:1-3; 2 PETER 1:9; ACTS 1:8).

He has an up-and-down spiritual experience.

He cannot understand himself—he wants to do what is right, but cannot.

He fails to draw upon the power of the Holy Spirit to live the Christian life.

(1 CORINTHIANS 3:1-3; ROMANS 7:15-24; 8:7; GALATIANS 5:16-18).

THE CARNAL MAN—Some or all of the following traits may characterize the Christian who does not fully trust God:

IGNORANCE OF HIS SPIRITUAL HERITAGE

IMPURE THOUGHTS

JEALOUSY

DISOBEDIENCE

LOSS OF LOVE FOR GOD AND FOR OTHERS

DISCOURAGEMENT

POOR PRAYER LIFE

NO DESIRE FOR BIBLE STUDY

LEGALISTIC ATTITUDE

UNBELIEF

GUILT

WORRY

CRITICAL SPIRIT

FRUSTRATION

AIMLESSNESS

(THE INDIVIDUAL WHO PROFESSES TO BE A CHRISTIAN BUT WHO CONTINUES TO PRACTICE SIN SHOULD REALIZE THAT HE MAY NOT BE A CHRISTIAN AT ALL, ACCORDING TO 1 JOHN 2:3; 3:6, 9; EPHESIANS 5:5).

The third truth gives us the only solution to this problem . . .

JESUS PROMISED THE ABUNDANT AND FRUITFUL LIFE AS THE RESULT OF BEING FILLED (CONTROLLED AND EMPOWERED) BY THE HOLY SPIRIT.

The Spirit-filled life is the Christ-controlled life by which Christ lives His life in and through us in the power of the Holy Spirit (JOHN 15).

One becomes a Christian through the ministry of the Holy Spirit, according to JOHN 3:1-8. From the moment of spiritual birth, the Christian is indwelt by the Holy Spirit at all times (JOHN 1:12; COLOSSIANS 2:9, 10; JOHN 14:16, 17). Though all Christians are indwelt by the Holy Spirit, not all Christians are filled (controlled and empowered) by the Holy Spirit.

The Holy Spirit is the source of the overflowing life (JOHN 7:37-39).

The Holy Spirit came to glorify Christ (JOHN 16:1-15). When one is filled with the Holy Spirit, he, too, will glorify Christ.

In His last command before His ascension, Christ promised the power of the Holy Spirit to enable us to be witnesses for Him (ACTS 1:1-9).

How, then, can one be filled with the Holy Spirit?

WE ARE FILLED (CONTROLLED AND EMPOWERED) BY THE HOLY SPIRIT BY FAITH; THEN WE CAN EXPERIENCE THE ABUNDANT AND FRUITFUL LIFE WHICH CHRIST PROMISED TO EACH CHRISTIAN.

You can appropriate the filling of the Holy Spirit right now if you:

Sincerely desire to be controlled and empowered by the Holy Spirit (MATTHEW 5:6;JOHN 7:37-39).

Confess your sins.

By faith thank God that He has forgiven all of your sins—past, present, and future—because Christ died for you (COLOSSIANS 2:13-15; 1 JOHN 1; 2: 1-3; HEBREWS 10:1-17).

By faith claim the fullness of the Holy Spirit, according to: HIS COMMAND—Be filled with the Spirit.

"And do not get drunk with wine, for that is dissipation, but be filled with the Spirit" (EPHESIANS 5:18).

HIS PROMISE—He will always answer when we pray according to His will.

"And this is the confidence which we have before Him, that if we ask anything according to His will, He hears us. And if we know that He hears us in whatever we ask, we know that we have the requests which we have asked from Him" (1 JOHN 5:14, 15).

Faith can be expressed through prayer . . .

HOW TO PRAY IN FAITH TO BE FILLED WITH THE HOLY SPIRIT

We are filled with the Holy Spirit by faith alone. However, true prayer is one way of expressing your faith. The following is a suggested prayer:

"Dear Father, I need You. I acknowledge that I have been in control of my life; and that, as a result, I have sinned against You. I thank You that You have forgiven my sins through Christ's death on the cross for me. I now invite Christ to again take control of the throne of my life. Fill me with the Holy Spirit as You commanded me to be filled, and as You promised in your Word that You would do if I asked in faith. I pray this in the name of Jesus. As an expression of my faith, I now thank You for taking control of my life and for filling me with the Holy Spirit."

Does this prayer express the desire of your heart? If so, bow in prayer and trust God to fill you with the Holy Spirit right now.

HOW TO KNOW THAT YOU ARE FILLED (CONTROLLED AND EMPOWERED) BY THE HOLY SPIRIT

Did you ask God to fill you with the Holy Spirit? Do you know that you are now filled with the Holy Spirit? On what authority? (On the trustworthiness of God Himself and His Word: **HEBREWS 11:6; ROMANS 14:22, 23**).

Do not depend upon feelings. The promise of God's Word, not our feelings, is our authority. The Christian lives by faith (trust) in the trustworthiness of God Himself and His Word. This train diagram illustrates the relationship between fact (God and His Word), faith (our trust in God and His Word), and feeling (the result of our faith and obedience) **(JOHN 14:21)**.

The train will run with or without the caboose. However, it would be futile to attempt to pull the train by the caboose. In the same way, we, as Christians, do not depend upon feelings or emotions, but we place our faith (trust) in the trustworthiness of God and the promises of His Word.

HOW TO WALK IN THE SPIRIT

Faith (trust in God and in His promise) is the only means by which a Christian can live the Spirit-controlled life. As you continue to trust Christ moment by moment:

Your life will demonstrate more and more of the fruit of the Spirit **(GALATIANS 5:22, 23)**; and will be more and more conformed to the image of Christ **(ROMANS 12:2; 2 CORINTHIANS 3:18)**.

Your prayer life and study of God's Word will become more meaningful.

You will experience His power in witnessing (**ACTS 1:8**).

You will be prepared for spiritual conflict against the world (**1 JOHN 2:15-17**); against the flesh (**GALATIANS 5:16, 17**); and against Satan (**1 PETER 5:7-9; EPHESIANS 6:10-13**).

You will experience His power to resist temptation and sin (**1 CORINTHIANS 10:13; PHILIPPIANS 4:13; EPHESIANS 1:19-23; 6:10; 2 TIMOTHY 1:7; ROMANS 6:1-6**).

SPIRITUAL BREATHING

BY FAITH YOU CAN CONTINUE TO EXPERIENCE GOD'S LOVE AND FORGIVENESS.

If you become aware of an area of your life (an attitude or an action) that is displeasing to the Lord, even though you are walking with Him and sincerely desiring to serve Him, simply thank God that He has forgiven your sins—past, present and future—on the basis of Christ's death on the cross. Claim His love and forgiveness by faith and continue to have fellowship with Him.

If you retake the throne of your life through sin—a definite act of disobedience—breathe spiritually.

Spiritual breathing (exhaling the impure and inhaling the pure) is an exercise in faith that enables you to continue to experience God's love and forgiveness.

Exhale—confess your sin—agree with God concerning your sin and thank him for His forgiveness of it, according to **1 JOHN 1:9** and **HEBREWS 10:1-25**. Confession involves repentance—a change in attitude and action.

Inhale—surrender the control of your life to Christ, and appropriate (receive) the fullness of the Holy Spirit by faith. Trust that He now controls and empowers you, according to the command of **EPHESIANS 5:18**, and the promise of **1 JOHN 5:14, 15**.

WORKS CITED

Albright, William F. **Archaeology and the Religion of Israel.** Baltimore: John Hopkins, 1942, p. 127-128. (Cited in *Meet My Head Coach*, p. 30).

DeBord, Sally. **"All the Lonely People."** Collegiate Challenge 10 1971. (Cited in *Meet My Head Coach,* p. 97).

Fromm, Erich. **The Art of Loving.** New York: Harper & Row, 1965, p. 50. (Cited in *Meet My Head Coach,* p. 98).

Gandhi, Mohandas. **All Men Are Brothers.** New York: Columbia U. and UNESCO, 1958. (Cited in *Meet My Head Coach*, p. 29).

Glassner, William. **Reality Therapy.** New York: Harper & Row, 1965, p. 9. (Cited in *Meet My Head Coach*, p. 92).

Glueck, Nelson. **Rivers in the Desert.** New York: Farrer, Straus Giroux, 1959, p. 31. (Cited in *Meet My Head Coach*, p. 30).

Lewis, C.S. **Mere Christianity.** London: Macmillan, Macmillan Paperbacks, 1952. (Cited in *Meet My Head Coach*, p. 29).

Maltz, Maxwell. **Psycho-Cybernetics.** New Jersey: Prentice-Hall, 1960, p. 55. (Cited in *Meet My Head Coach,* p. 141).

Ibid., p. 39. (Cited in *Meet My Head Coach*, p. 140).

Ibid., p. 111. (Cited in *Meet My Head Coach*, p. 141).

Peterson, J.A. **Who Runs Your Life?** Lincoln, Nebraska: Good News Broadcasting, 1967. (Cited in *Meet My Head Coach*, p. 109).

A CONVERSATION WITH GOD

My Dearest Father, You have allowed me the privilege of viewing firsthand Your 39-year loving process with a man; and to You, God, I am most grateful. That man is Fred Crowell. Thank you for pursuing him and moving him *"by a path his feet have not traveled before,"* just like You have done with the nations of this world (ISAIAH 41:3). What an incredible journey!

Now, with the process seen clearly in retrospect, we can say Your way has been perfect. There have been times both of us have come close to allowing the "wiggle room" to overtake us. Yet as a loving, tender shepherd, You have carried Fred Crowell, myself and NBC Camps *"close to Your heart"* (ISAIAH 40:11). Certainly, life became more exciting when Fred gave You permission to chart his course. You are taking him where others have never gone before and where he never thought he could go . . . yes, beyond anything he could even ask or think, beyond his wildest dreams. You have taken some of the smallest events and turned them into momentous events in his history.

God, I thank You also for placing Fred Crowell in my Hall of Faith, along with Noah, Abraham, Joseph, Moses and others, who wisely stayed the course and found their fulfilling purpose in the process. As with all of these, and also in the game of basketball, I have seen at times Your way includes practice, paying the price, pain, perseverance—processes most of us would not choose.

Dear God, I can't help but wonder *what if* Fred had resisted Your way of bringing this life about, as most of us are prone to do? *What if* he had surrendered to the god of becoming the "winningest" coach, of financial security, of physical health, or of power of position? *What if* he had misread Your ways in his life when tempted?

Undoubtedly, many young campers would not know how to best chart their course through life. Probably, my beloved husband at seventy years of age would not have written to me, "thank you for staying with me until I found Jesus." And, most likely, all NBC Camps staff would not be as intently a light in their darkened world of influence.

My praise goes to You, my God, *"so that people may see and know, may consider and understand, that the hand of the Lord has done this. . ."* (ISAIAH 41:20). And I ask You, in Your supreme and sovereign mercy, to grant Fred Crowell many more years of leadership.

M. GAIL WRIGHT

BORN AND RAISED IN SEATTLE, WASHINGTON, GAIL WRIGHT RESIDES WITH HER HUSBAND CLARY IN SPOKANE. SINCE 1968, SHE HAS CONTRIBUTED TO FRED CROWELL'S PROFESSIONAL LIFE IN ACCOUNTING AND ADMINISTRATION. GAIL RECEIVED HER BACHELOR OF MUSIC DEGREE FROM WHEATON COLLEGE IN CHICAGO; SHE USED HER MUSICAL GIFT TEACHING PRIVATE PIANO AND AS AN ACCOMPANIST IN SPOKANE.